Torque

to the End of

the World

by

Mark Wadie

©2018 Mark Wadie

All Rights Reserved.

Introduction

I am in a small cottage down on the South coast of the Isle of Man. It is colder than Africa, which is where I have been living for the past few years, but it is a good quiet location I think, for starting to write this book.

I think – because I haven't done it before. Write a book that is!

I've done plenty of 'thinking'.

To be honest it feels a bit like starting to do homework,

Why do homework when I don't need to?

The only reason is because I have been sprinkled with basically two sentences over the last thirty years or so, 'Have you ever thought of writing a book?' and 'You should write a book!'

I could keep delaying it I suppose, but at the end of the day it is probably a suitable time in my life, to get stuck in and obey the prompting. Having recently come back to live in England, it seems a good time to reflect and write before I get stuck into the next phase of life.

So, thanks to Charles and Jana for the cottage. Now it's up to me, to start this thing and see where it goes.

In the animated film 'Finding Nemo', there is a scene where Nemo's Dad (who is a clown fish) comes across a bale of turtles going on a long trip in a strong Atlantic sea current and there is an invitation given to Nemo's Dad who is also going that way, but has never done anything like – going with such a current.

The invite to him from a friendly turtle, is this, 'Grab shell dude!'

So, as I 'grab shell'... I hope you grab shell too... and we both enjoy the adventure together.

1959

There were a couple of lovers. I guess they were lovers. I hope they were lovers, else it's not so good.

I have never met them.

Their names are Stephen, who is a Greek Cypriot, and Gwynne, who is Welsh. Stephen is a tailor, living in the South East of England. They are both in their early twenties. They meet. And at some point, they have sex. I do know this – because I exist!

1960

The result of that union meant I hung out in a womb until Saturday 9th July. What went on in that womb might not have been so nice.

I only know this because of something which happened to me over twenty years later. (I will probably tell you all about it, if you keep grabbing shell.)

But I was out and that was the main thing. Better out than in.

I came out in a hospital in London. Gwynne stayed with me for about three weeks or so I think. Then she had to leave London to get on with her life. She only went to London to get me out of the womb where no one would know about it all going on. Sometimes mothers had to do that sort of thing back then.

She must have been scared and feeling quite lonely at this time and was in a very difficult situation in her life. She also struggled with leaving me, knowing that she could never return.

I know this because of one sentence: 'When I think of Colin, it still makes me cry.' She put that in a letter to the adoption agency later that year, and I got hold of the letter many years later.

She called me Colin. But that was a long time ago.

Anyway, that sort of thing leaves hidden scars in mothers and babies. Because it's a big thing to separate a mother and baby. You can't get away with it without damage to both. Those first weeks or months are where a baby learns to t.r.u.s.t, also where it learns to receive. It's a bit of a struggle if that primary foundation isn't in place. But of course, a baby can't put all that sort of stuff into words. It can't even talk!

That's all about intimate stuff anyway, it's hard enough to make sense of, even when the baby turns into an adult.

So, the baby has to put those needs down deep inside somewhere. It's got other needs to think about, like food, drink and warmth. And some external safety if it comes along, because unless those things come along, he or she is a goner!

And in my case, I was about four weeks old so there was no way I was going to conjure up my own food, drink, warmth and safety.

So it needed to come along. And in my case. It did.

There were actually two people who came along to help my situation and by helping my situation it also helped their situation. So it was a good match. Makes me think of that old saying: 'a match made in heaven'. But who believes in that sort of thing these days!

It helped those two people because they had been struggling and failing to create a baby of their own. So having an opportunity to care for someone else's baby obviously was the way forward for them. And that's what they did.

They took me on board.

His name was Timothy and he was working for the Merchant Navy at the time and her name was Pamela and she was working as a nurse. Now, this couple were married to each other and their surname was Wadie.

In August of that year Tim and Pam took me from London to their home in Salfords, Surrey.

A few months later they legally adopted me as their child. The Three of us were now a family. That's better!

So now I was to have a surname the same as theirs and it was they who also gave me my permanent first name. My new name was to be Mark. Good name that!

Mark means Mighty Warrior.

They also gave me a middle name for what it's worth: Stephen. I might remember to tell you what Stephen means or stands for later in the book. For now it's a secret, unless you already know of course!

But I will tell you what Wadie means because it sort of fits the first name they gave me. Wadie means, 'to snatch victory in battle'.

Now Tim and Pam didn't know that those names carried those meanings, even I only found it out many years later but I think names are important so I'm happy I was named Mark Wadie.

The Swingin' Sixties

Now the swinging hippy sixties were obviously going on when I was on planet Earth, but when they were, my age was not even in double figures, so I had different things going on. Like nappies, walking, infant school and even a dose of junior school.

Tim and Pam also had new names not known to either of them in the Fifties. They now had the privileged names respectively of Daddy and Mummy.

The three of us lived, as I said earlier, in a small village in Surrey called Salfords, on a small road called Honeycrock Lane. Then soon after my 2nd birthday someone else turned up in the family. A baby girl. My parents called her Julie. She also was adopted.

Guess when her birthday was?

July 9th. Same as mine. Funny old world isn't it?

One thing I still remember about living in the house on Honeycrock Lane is the event of my 3rd birthday and Julie's 1st birthday.

I remember coming downstairs to see my new birthday present and Julie's present. They were pretty good presents back in those days. Nowadays some serious money gets dished out for children's birthday presents. But back then there was less 'stuff' about.

Julie had a straw stuffed dog on wheels that she could push about as she learned to walk. It wasn't a real dog that had been stuffed – just a toy one!

Mum, Dad, Julie and me, plus stuffed straw dog

And I had a blue metal pedal police car... to help me learn to drive. That's funny!

Suffice to say... I do remember those presents.

In about 1964 Mum and Dad moved to a new house three miles south of Salfords. It was on the outskirts of Horley, near Gatwick airport.

It was a detached house on two acres of land down a road called Peaks Brook Lane.

We were near the end of the lane next to some stables and a tributary to the River Mole.

It was a wonderful place to grow up as a child. One acre was slowly transformed by my parents into flower beds, vegetable garden, rockery and lawn, with about a dozen fruit trees on it.

The other acre was left as a field and was used by the local stables to graze a couple of their horses on. In exchange for that use, they allowed Julie and I to have free riding lessons on a regular basis. Also Dad picked up all the horse poo into his wheelbarrow and used it as fertiliser on the vegetable garden and flower beds. Free poo... wouldn't have got that if the horses had been stuffed and pushed about on wheels!

As for the free riding lessons – that was basically a joy for Julie and she went on to love horses for many years. For me – I could have done without it. Too high up for my liking. Plus they had a mind of their own, which wasn't conducive to me feeling comfortable or safe.

One particular event that stands out in my mind was when I was in a field on one of the horses, trotting around in a circle with other horses and riders. The stable owner, Mr. Jepson, who was in the middle of the circle cracked his big whip to get my horse to go faster. My horse charged off from the circle full blast to the edge of the field towards a barbed wire fence. I was terrified. Totally out of control. The horse managed to stop just before it ran into the fence. I'm so glad it didn't jump the fence, else I might still be on it today. What a life that would have been!

And that was enough for me to definitely know I didn't like horse riding. Julie loved it though and was the master of the horse, rather than the other way round. Which was always my problem... anyway I digress.

I was about four years old when we moved to that house in Peaks Brook Lane. The house was named Ellerton. It was certainly very exciting to have such a big garden as a small child, and the fun got better when Dad built a small tree house in a small sycamore tree and hung a sit-on rope swing from another sycamore tree. He also bought a few pets. Cindy the dog (live!), Popper the cat and Peter the rabbit. Can't remember which ones came first, but they all occurred during our time at that house.

A continual event at Ellerton was passenger aeroplanes flying over as they descended to land at Gatwick Airport. The planes flew very low just near to the end of our property. You could read what was written on the sides of them easily. It got me looking up a lot.

I used to love lying on the lawn looking up at the sky and watching the clouds change shape. Big fluffy clouds with a deep blue backdrop. Loved doing that.

I also loved playing football with my Dad in the garden. Could not get enough of it. I used to dream of being a famous footballer. It wasn't realistic, but my dreams told me it was. So I stayed in my dreams a lot.

Our family transport at this time was a 250cc Sunbeam scooter with a sidecar. Julie and me were in the side-car with Mum and

Dad rode the scooter. Although occasionally Mum also rode the bike.

Around the mid Sixties Dad bought a white Vauxhall Victor car to get the four of us about in.

Then life changed – in 1965, I hit five years old. And this thing happened that I had not known about before. It was called school. (Dun dun dun...!) I remember the first day. It was horrible. Being away from home and my parents for the whole day, with loads of people I didn't know. I asked my Mum at the end of the day, 'How many more days do I have to go to school?' And she said, 'Just over ten years.'

What the heck was that all about? It couldn't be true. That was forever.

I'm sure I cried quite a lot.

I obviously couldn't do anything about it and ended up doing my time! But I would have preferred not to.

I remember one particularly horrible day at Albert Road Infant School when at 9 a.m. my mum dropped me off outside the school. It had been raining and an overflow pipe was pouring out rain water. As I entered the playground, this older boy who I didn't know ran up to me and took my school cap off. He then held it under the overflow pipe. Kids were laughing I'm sure. Well my Mum had seen it happen and was furious and chased after the boy, who escaped into the school building. It was a humiliating experience, and didn't help me enjoy school any more than I had before.

Of course, much worse things have happened to kids at school.

But on that day I was trapped in my own bubble of embarrassment and I record it as part of my school journey.

Me at infant school

I never really liked playtimes at school. Too much unruly behaviour. For whatever reason I tended to have a more quiet and sensitive nature.

I liked playing football and other games with kids, but kids have other sides to them as well… nice ones. I liked the sense of belonging when the atmosphere was good, but then you also have all the intimidating status/power agendas. That's the stuff I didn't like. So it could get lonely on the playground sometimes. I didn't fit in. And in that sense, I didn't belong. I'm sure there must have been plenty of other kids feeling the same as me.

When I was around eight years old I moved up to Lumley Road Junior School. Not much changed, just bigger kids were around.

But my parents encouraged me to join Cub Scouts, and although quite daunting at first I got to enjoy Cubs. The discipline was better (better adult to child ratio), so there was less unruly behaviour. Also there were things like triangular badges to earn that could be sewn onto your sleeve as a merit of accomplishment. There were many different proficiency badges to obtain such as cookery, troubadour, camping skills, fire building, knot tying skills, sports and many others.

I liked being in Cubs and looked forward to going along one evening a week. I was in the '7th Horley, Burstow' pack.

It was well organised and was never boring, with fun games and other activities to occupy us.

My parents also took us to church most Sunday mornings. Now that was boring, but the Sunday school halfway through the service (which we went in another room for) was occasionally good. But it never reached the heights of fun that Cubs did.

In 1968 another person joined our family. He was also adopted. My parents named him Robert.

Now we were five.

Three children with unknown history, all brought together under the banner of the Wadie family.

Dad stopped going to sea when we were quite young because it was not conducive with family life I guess. He could and would have become a ship Captain with the P&O New Zealand Shipping Company. He was already second officer on the ships he sailed with.

So it was a big step for him to leave his life at sea. A sacrifice he made to be a father.

He went on to work for the same shipping company, but at their offices in London. His job was to arrange the loading of the cargo onto ships. He cycled each day to Horley Station and commuted from there by train to the P&O offices in London.

Life at home was sometimes scary. There were arguments, especially at weekends. Often after we had gone to bed. There were obviously some unresolved issues under the surface.

I speak now as an adult of course because such concepts were unknown to me as a young boy.

But the arguments were sometime very loud and distressing for both Julie and I and we would creep into each other's bed, cry and try to cover our ears. All this uncertainty in our parents relationship was probably also tapping into our already weakened sense of security from being rejected by our birth parents.

The arguments were never physical, but at times things were thrown across the room and smashed. And that made it even more frightening for us because it seemed like things were getting totally out of control.

I think bringing up three kids who were not their own was part of it, but under all of that was probably the feeling of perceived shame and inadequacy from not being able to produce kids of their own.

It was Mum who apparently was unable to bear children and this was obviously a sore topic. But, I was to find out many years later that this was not actually the case!

Very occasionally, Julie and I were the recipients of the tensions going on. Especially if we were being out of order. One comment that popped up when things got out of hand was, 'If it wasn't for us, you kids would still be in the gutter.' It was a poignant thing to say and who knows how we received that sort of comment, but life goes on.

There was probably also financial stress around that time which tends to rattle the cage and bring out underlying insecurities in people.

But whatever all the issues were, it reveals that living out in the country with a nice garden is not always a bed of roses.

Yet, Mum and Dad had many times of fun and laughing too. They set up a net on the grass and played tennis, they really enjoyed gardening together, they played board games together and also with us, which we loved, plus they took us on many adventures.

They were also planning a different working lifestyle for themselves.

Dad was writing a book called 'The Commuter' (a novel), he later tried writing another book (also a novel) about drug smuggling on ships.

He then tried writing short stories, but all the efforts he made to try and get these books published failed.

He was also trying to get a screen-printing business started – printing hundreds of pens with various company names on them for people. This project failed.

They also tried creative things like making table lights with empty bottles. That didn't take off either.

But the one thing that ended up being the way forward for their working lives was when Mum started going to a weekly evening catering course in Croydon.

They were planning one day to leave the South East and start a catering business of some sort. I was still a young boy so wasn't aware of their thinking and planning.

Another treat for us at Ellerton was having a TV. It was only black and white, as colour TVs were very rare back then, but what a treat for us kids. 'Watch with Mother' was my first favourite TV programme. Then as I got a bit older, things like 'Batman and Robin', 'Skippy', 'Flipper' and my most favourite of all 'Lost in Space'. I used to so look forward to the next episode that carried on from the cliff-hanger ending (always a dramatic moment) of the week before. Fridays was the night. Loved it.

My Mum and Dad used to watch grown up programmes like 'Panorama', 'World in Action', 'The News at 10' and 'Monty Python's Flying Circus'. One programme they especially liked was 'The Good Life', a weekly comedy drama about a couple who were determined to be self-sufficient and live off the land.

I think that was the life Mum and Dad really aspired too. It inspired them – but it was not to be. Another special memory from the Sixties were the trips to our Grandparents. Dad's parents were living in Newenden, 35 miles from Tunbridge Wells in Kent. I particularly enjoyed spending time with dad in the car on the journey there and back.

When I reached the age of nine, I was allowed to mow the lawn at the front and rear of their house, which was out in the country. I loved doing that, just me and Dad together for the day.

The mower was a petrol driven rotary blade model that made the lawn look pretty in rows.

One day I was trying to turn the mower off so I could go in for lunch, by earthing out the spark plug with a strip of metal that was there for cutting out the engine. As I was pushing the strip of metal down onto the spark plug I felt what I thought was my Dad hitting me hard on my back with his hand. The engine was still running and making the usual engine din and I thought he was cross with me about something because it was a big hard slap on the back.

When I turned round to see why he had hit me so hard there was no one there!

I couldn't understand what was going on, so I ran inside to talk to Dad about it. He came outside and when I explained this unusual event he laughed and explained to me that I had just had an electric shock from the HT lead to the spark plug. That was a new experience for me. Quite invigorating, once I had got over the shock! (Ba-bum!) Must have got my heart going better!

My other Grandparents, on my mum's side, lived behind the 'John Bull' Rubber factory on Gwendolen Road, in Leicester.

I particularly liked hanging out with this Grandpa. He took me out on car trips in his little Ford Anglia and he always had a pack of chewy Murray mints or Fox's Glacier mints in the glove box. He also took me pond fishing a few times, which was a new experience that involved him teaching me how to put maggots and worms on hooks to see if we could tempt a fish to bite. I never caught anything big, but it started an interest in me that was put to use a few years later.

Then there was the interest that took me through my school years.

It started in 1969 when I was nine years old. Grandpa took me to see my first professional football game. He had played a few times for Gillingham when he was younger, but it was not Gillingham we went to see, it was Leicester City.

Leicester City were in the old second division (which is now called the Championship League), and the day I went to see them play at Filbert Street ground, they were playing Oxford United.

In those days it was nearly all standing room only… on the terraces, and the place was full and very noisy and quite intimidating when you are short and nine years old. Fully grown men crammed together shouting and singing, and sometimes the whole mass would sway forward and take me off my feet like a big sea wave overpowering me.

But I was with my Grandpa. So it was OK. Well, Leicester won 2 – 1 and I was from then on, a Leicester supporter. I went a few more times to the Filbert Street ground when we were in Leicester visiting Mum's parents. I went with various older family members if Leicester were playing at home. I saw John Toshack play for Cardiff against Leicester before he went onto join Liverpool. My grandpa pointed him out and told me he was a good player and would go onto greater things, which he did.

So anything to do with Leicester City over the next few years got my interest.

Unfortunately they never really achieved much over the next few years, but it never stopped me daydreaming to the contrary. Oh, did I daydream!

Daydreaming was a regular hobby as a kid. It was often mentioned in my end of term school reports. Nice of them to notice!

Another big event to happen in 1969, which resulted in fifty people dying, occurred at 1.30am on Sunday 5th January. A Boeing 727 passenger aeroplane crashed into a detached house at the end of our lane.

There was a couple in the house at the time with their baby.

The house was demolished. I still remember riding past on a horse later that day and seeing the big plane mangled up with its tail in the air.

The report that came out blamed the pilot for the fatal crash. There was also thick heavy fog that night.

Forty eight people on the plane were killed. Fourteen survived.

The couple in the house died but amazingly a policeman who was on traffic duty nearby rushed to the scene and managed to rescue the baby from the demolished house. Apparently he found the child underneath its upturned cot, which had protected it.

The plane had come short of the Gatwick runway by just over a mile.

Julie had said when she woke up in the morning that she had heard the sound of Daleks in the night. It was probably the emergency crew megaphones that she heard. We only found out about the accident when Mum's sister Margaret phoned us in the morning to see if we were still alive. Strange how disaster can be so nearby and we are oblivious to it.

So this is the general shape of the first ten years of my life. A few other key memories that I haven't mentioned from those years are as follows:

- Bonfires in the field and the smell of burning wood and leaves.
- Family firework displays.
- The smell of newly cut grass.
- Cycling with Julie on our bikes down muddy bumpy lanes near our house.
- Conkers.
- Marbles.
- Dressing up as Cowboys and Indians with Julie.
- Camping trips with the family.
- Camping trips with the Cub scouts – especially the one in the Lake District.
- Running away from home – but only reaching the end of the field because it was too big a thing to go any further. I was upset about something Julie had done.
- Going to the cinema and seeing films like, 'Chitty Chitty Bang Bang' (I so wanted to be in that family) and other films like 'Aristocats', '101 Dalmatians' and 'Jungle Book'. These were special new films that had come out and they were in colour too. Amazing. So special.
- Learning to fix bicycles.
- Christmas at our Grandparents.
- Christmas at home.
- Christmas anywhere.
- Trying to do small magic performances.
- Collecting things: football cards, coins, stamps and much more!

- Finding or seeing or catching small animals, birds or insects.
- Action Man.
- Snow. Loved it. So exciting.
- Electric power cuts – used to happen in the Sixties sometimes. Then we needed candles. So exciting.
- Thunderstorms, although a bit scary...
- Migrating birds on the telegraph wires by our house waiting to leave England for the winter. Hundreds of them, for days on end. Then. All gone.
- Talking secretly to Cindy our dog who would listen to every word I said. Much of my loneliness and general confusion about life was shared with Cindy. You can't do that with a stuffed dog on wheels!
- But come to think of it... another strong memory is telling my teddy when I went to bed, all the events of the day – good and bad. In fact that teddy heard more from my heart on a regular basis than Cindy did. Hopefully one of them understood and cared about me!

(Hey this childhood memory stuff is good therapy. I think I might stay with it a bit longer. Just skip to the next chapter if it gets boring. I won't take it personally. Just don't tell me.)

Me, Robert and Julie near the end of the Sixties

- During my time at Junior School I wrote a twenty-seven-page story in green ink called 'The Magic Elephant '. He went all round the world on adventures. My teacher was so impressed by the length of it that she asked me to read it to the class.

- Hating going to Crawley swimming pool with the school.

- Farmer Crompton's cows breaking into our garden after escaping from his nearby farm fields – which were not properly fenced. They did so much damage to the lawn and the flower beds. It happened quite a lot. Heart-breaking for my Mum and Dad after their ongoing care of the garden.

- Dreaming of going down the nearby small river in a hand-built raft, and the adventure of discovering where it all went.

- Liking a girl called Amanda at Junior school and then seeing her walking with a schoolmate called Ian near Horley Railway Station from the rear car window as I was being taken home from school.

- She probably liked him. She didn't even know I liked her. Life can be rubbish sometimes.

- Julie telling Dad that I liked a girl called Amanda. Then my Dad laughing at the thought of a boy of nine years old fancying a girl. I felt totally embarrassed and humiliated. Could life get any worse??

(I'm remembering all sorts here! If you're still with me that is?)

- Having an unhealthy fascination with the topic of Francis Dashwood and the 'Hellfire' club in High Wycombe. It had started when our family were driving through High Wycombe when I was about eight or nine and I saw a strange golden domed temple on a hill. My Dad told me what it was and I ended up doing a small study on it all.

- Learning to play chess.

- Seeing a long name on a bicycle owned by the older brother of my friend Kevin (he lived next door in the house of the stables owner). The name on the bicycle was 'Mephistopheles'. Kevin told me the name meant 'messenger of the devil'. I never forgot that word it seems, because it cropped up in my memory ten years later and became a significant name for a few years. I will tell you all about it later. (Grab shell dude!)

- Indoor fireworks, when the weather was too bad on fireworks night. There was such a thing as indoor fireworks. Not as big as the outdoor ones though!

- Having a small bag of crisps once a week. Tuesdays it was. When Mr. Moat the grocer came round in his van.

- Dr Who and the Daleks. Even in Black and White it was scary. It was those voices.

- Oast houses in Kent.

- Going up the Post Office Tower on a family trip.

- On a school trip to London, watching a procession and seeing the Queen go past in the back of her car.

- Going to Goodwood race meeting with the family. Pretty sure Lester Piggott (the famous jockey) was on one of the horses.

- Oh, I just remembered one of my most exciting times as a child! It was a yearly family event run by Dad's shipping company colleagues. It was at a mansion somewhere with big grounds. It was only for families from the company, so it wasn't crowded or anything. But oh, what a day. Everything was free. Ice cream and cones, donkey rides, Punch and Judy shows, fairground activities like merry go rounds, skittles, running competitions. The place was buzzing and I could just wander about on my own if I wanted, as could Julie, and we could go on anything, eat anything, drink anything, enjoy anything... for free!

I forgot about those memories! I never wanted those days (held once a year) to end. There was so much to do. Nothing like Disneyland I suppose – but I am easily pleased. And those days at Dad's yearly event were the best ever.

Suppose I had better stop remembering, else I will get stuck in the Sixties. Plus that was a good memory to end on.

1970

A new decade, and life for me was going to change in many ways. I was even going to become an adult – by age at least!

But let's start at the beginning of the Seventies.

I was still living at Ellerton, near Horley. The next-door neighbour Kevin, who I mentioned earlier, was around more often these days. He was a couple of years older than me but he seemed fine hanging out with Julie and me which was good.

I remember a tramp's shack burnt down very near our home and the three of us went to explore the burnt-out shell. I found a chest of drawers all burnt and when I looked inside I found a wooden chess set (only one bishop was missing!). It was Kevin who then taught me to play chess.

Anyway the three of us liked exploring and looking for adventures. Kevin's dad worked in nearby Crawley for an engineering company called 'Woodall-Duckham', and he had given Kevin three blue metal lapel badges from his company with the letters WD on them.

So Kevin, Julie and I started up a little club of our own called 'Wood Detectives' seeing as we had woods all round where we lived. And we each had our own lapel badge. What we didn't have were many incidents that needed three young detectives. But that did not deter us! We had a secret club, we had a badge and we had regular meetings to create projects for our secret club.

Around this time, a rather large interruption was happening at the end of our garden and alongside our previously quiet Peaks Brook Lane.

And this interruption, or should I say invasion, was the start of a very large engineering project. And that project was the building of the M23 motorway!

The end of our garden, literally just over the hedge, was to be the location of Junction 9 of the M23 (complete with roundabout). This was the junction that would take traffic the short distance to the Gatwick airport complex.

So there was a lot of activity all around our homes.

But, back to the 'Wood Detectives'!

We decided to make a bit of money for ourselves. We made bottles of orange squash and carried the bottles and some cups onto the huge muddy motorway site. We would walk amongst the workers selling cups or whole bottles of squash to anyone who was thirsty. And we did well. We used to have a secret dug out hole in the ground at our base where we would keep the squash cool.

And on these trips to the workers (at the weekend and in the school holidays) we became friends with the main foreman chap. He was called 'Chin' and he was Chinese. He was a really nice guy and in the end he took the three of us in his work Land Rover along the muddy trail of the motorway site, where we would meet other workers who we sold our orange squash to.

And believe it or not he eventually let Kevin and I sit on his lap and steer the Land Rover. These days he would probably get arrested for that sort of thing and for more reasons than one!

But it was all totally innocent and safe. We used to love going off in that Land Rover. It was so exciting for us kids.

The prospect of the new motorway on the horizon and the ever-increasing volume of air traffic to Gatwick must have been at the foremost of my parents minds as they thought and planned about the future.

But for now they were staying put.

1971

This was the year of BIG school!

It was to be Balcombe Road Secondary School.

And this was to be even more daunting because there were even bigger boys at secondary school and there were all sorts of rumours about what they would do to first year pupils like us. It really did concern me. But what could I do?

Thankfully the rumours did not materialise. Yet, I still found the whole scene very intimidating and never really felt relaxed at this new school.

To make matters worse there was a bully in my year. He had come from the same Junior school as me and had developed into being a ruffian. He was going to a boxing club in Crawley and also he had an elder brother at the school so he was in quite a good position as far as his sense of security went, and I guess it went to his head.

Well this guy was known to be my friend and he seemed to want to be my friend, but he was no friend. He was a tormenter who enjoyed intimidating me with his violent streak.

He also intimidated a lot of other people in our year.

1972

I used to look forward to the weekends. Kevin, Julie and I were still roaming around as 'Wood Detectives' and the Motorway was still underway.

I had now joined the Scouts, which is the next step up from the Cubs. It was not quite as enjoyable, probably because in the Cubs I was one of the oldest and had been made leader of a newly formed team in our Pack, and I was enjoying that position; but it was short-lived, as I had reached the age where I had to leave and join the 7th Horley Burstow, Scout Troop.

The other Scouts were older than me, so that was also intimidating. But not as intimidating as Secondary School, because School was five days a week and it was a lot bigger than my Scout Troop.

There were a lot of good people in my class at school though. By the time I was in 2nd year I got to make a few friends. One of them was called Steven. He was a good guy and I used to lend him my bike to cycle home for lunch. In fact he used to give me some money each time he borrowed it from me. Nice little earner!

My lunch money for school each day was 12 pence and sometimes I would not eat lunch and instead save the money for sweets. 12 pence could buy 3 Mars bars in those days. And the Mars bars were bigger back then too! Or maybe my mouth was smaller. It's hard to tell.

After school sometimes bully boy used to go down the street with me and a boy called Robert to the local sweet shop. The old man who owned the shop had many big jars of different sweets. It was a classic old sweet shop. I never really felt comfortable with bully boy there but had to let him tag along to keep him sweet, if you know what I mean.

Someone else who I liked sitting next to in class ended up becoming famous. His name was Simon Gallup and in 1979 he joined the world-famous band 'The Cure' as their bass guitarist.

He and the singer Robert Smith are the only original members of the band who are still touring to this day.

When we used to hang out at school he used to tell me about Alice Cooper, who was Simon's older brother's hero. In the 70's Alice Cooper was one of the big names in music and used stage drama as part of his concerts, using things like guillotines and fake blood. He ended up becoming a born-again Christian and he still tours the world and has a big following, even now.

But I first heard about Alice Cooper from Simon, while we were in class together.

This year was my best football-playing year. I was centre-half in the Scout team and we reached the local Scout league cup final. I had a cold on the day of the final and thought I would not be well enough to play, but before I left home to go to the ground, my Dad encouraged me to run around our field a couple of times so that I would get some energy into me. He told me I would be well enough to play.

I ended up playing but we lost 2 – 1. I can't remember doing anything important in the game. To be honest I don't think I was a very good player. I scored amazing goals in my daydreams, but any scored in real life were few and far between; however I was in the team that reached the final. So I did achieve that.

Only the winners received medals. Bit harsh!

My other achievement, small as it was, was reaching the four-a-side football final at school. The tournament was for the First and Second year pupils. I was the goalkeeper in my class team and the matches were played in the gym over a period of days and weeks. It was a knock-out system and I was in the B team for my class. Bully boy was a good footballer and he was in the A team for our class.

Somehow the A team got knocked out in the earlier stages but our B team, kept winning. The day of the final arrived and we were in it playing some other A team from another class in our year. We ended up flamin' winning!

And we each got a medal. Come on!

I should also say that bully boy was encouraging us all the way and was happy that we did well.

But there were other times that he didn't make my life happy. As I said before he was a boxer and enjoyed intimidation. He would often threaten to beat me up and he did one time, he hit me hard in the face and broke my front tooth. Other times he would tell me to stay at home and pretend to be sick, otherwise he would do something to me. Most of my concerns about life at that time involved him. It was a secret that I kept from my parents.

I don't want to tell you some of the other incidents that went on during this year because I don't want to use up valuable space when I know that there are so many more dramatic and life-changing events to write about later in this book.

But in those days I used to dream of having a big strong older brother who would stand up for me.

I felt very alone in my struggles.

1973

Then the year of escape came knocking at my door and who was I to turn it down. Well I had no other choice as it happened.

Which was also fine by me!

Mum and Dad were about to carry out their own escape, so it was another match made in heaven as it were!

They had been looking for properties to buy in the Devon area of England. They were well aware that Ellerton was going to very soon be a totally different place, with the M23 right on their doorstep, and also the ever-increasing air traffic that was inevitable due to Gatwick being the 2nd largest airport in England and growing all the time.

They also wanted a different work style like I mentioned before. It was to be in the hospitality trade, which of course included catering. Hence the reason Mum had been attending her evening class in Croydon.

So they were on a mission for which they pulled out all the stops.

They eventually set their hearts on a small hotel/restaurant in a small town called Chudleigh, between Exeter and Plymouth. So it was on the main road for holidaymakers going through Devon to get to Cornwall.

As things turned out, road projects were to become a bit of a blight for Mum and Dad! But more of that later.

The main thing from my point of view was getting out of my personal little hellhole. Bully boy land.

There was obviously a lot for Mum and Dad to sort out with this big step into something new. One of those things was to organise the sale of my Grandparents' house in Kent, because around this time also, Dad's Dad had died – leaving his mum alone and in need of help. My grandmother was coming up to 80 around this time.

She would be moving with us to Chudleigh.

She wasn't the only one moving to Chudleigh with us either. Mum and Dad had been in discussions with Mum's aunt (her Dad's sister) who was also living in Leicester. Auntie Marjorie was also going to come and live in the Chudleigh Hotel and be a business partner. And also coming along for the ride was her daughter Susan who was seventeen and due to start a University course later in the year.

So it was all change. The adventure was about to begin.

The sale of our 4-bedroom house eventually got agreed at the sum of £21,000. But the 7-bedroomed Hotel in Devon was selling for £35,000. The price difference was bigger than my parents had hoped for and I think this fact reinforced the decision to include Auntie Marjorie in the project. They could share the burden of financial responsibility together.

The only regret for me at this time was leaving our good friend Kevin from next door. The 'Wood Detectives' were to disband! But strangely enough seven years later I was to start a new club and my association with Kevin played a part in what I would call it. But more of that later!

In late March of 1973 the day came to follow the sun west into a whole new life.

Dad had bought a Red Ford Cortina Mk2 a few weeks beforehand to replace the old White Vauxhall Victor. Mum and Dad picked me up from school in the Cortina and left the Vauxhall Victor with Mr Pentecost (my geography teacher). He paid them £5 I think. The school were going to use it as a vehicle to work on and teach pupils mechanical skills.

So the five of us drove out of the school grounds that day on route to our new home. I was nearly thirteen years old, Julie was nearly eleven and Robert was five.

As we drove out of the school gate there were two boys from my class who were around to wave goodbye. One of them was bully boy! Oh how I enjoyed my final goodbye wave to him.

I felt such a freedom. And that is not an exaggeration!

I now lived in Devon. Chudleigh was a small town and 'Orchard House Hotel' which was our new home was a large house in a terrace near the top of Old Exeter Street. It was one of two hotels in the town and was just off the main street.

My immediate project was to try and find out about the Chudleigh youth football team. I did find out about it and went and watched them but they were all older than me and it became apparent I was not suitable. If I had been a really good footballer I probably would have fitted in. But like I mentioned before – I wasn't. Apart from in my daydreams!

So fitting in was not going to come easy.

There was only one school in Chudleigh at the time and it was a Junior School, so that was where Julie was to go until later in the year when she would be old enough for Secondary School.

The nearest secondary school to us was in Kingsteignton a few miles away and near to Newton Abbot. So that is where I was to attend. There was a big fifty-two seater school bus that used to take Chudleigh kids to and from Kingsteignton Secondary School each day. The bus company was called 'Snells' and I remember the driver having Radio Two on as he drove.

So there was a whole load of new kids and I was the new boy, in the second year. There were also older kids in the bus. They used to sit in the back seats like they do. There were a few who were quite intimidating, but none of it compared to the close range bully boy antics at the Horley Secondary School.

So there was more air to breathe.

The first day I walked into the playground at the new school a guy about my age walked straight up to me and said, 'Hi I'm Jerry'. I said 'Hi' back and that was it. He was called Jeremy Wotton and he was the toughest guy in the year it turned out. But he was quite a friendly sort of guy. He was the guy who was the fastest at running and the best at sports and he was a bit bigger than most of the kids in our year.

It wasn't that me and him became good friends or anything but that friendly introduction put me at ease on that first day.

Bit by bit I made a couple of friends at school. Later in the year I went up to the 3rd year (it is called year nine now I think). And Julie was old enough now to enter the 1st year (year seven).

I was happy she was now in the same school as me, it gave me a greater sense of security somehow. Julie was a force to be reckoned with, she had less fear than me. And she would stand up for me. So she became like an older brother of sorts!

Life back at the Hotel was getting into some kind of rhythm. Dad was the frontman of course. He ran the little bar that was attached to the small restaurant and would take the food orders. Mum was in the kitchen cooking with Auntie Marjorie. My gran was doing the washing up and 17-year-old Susan was the waitress.

It wasn't that busy really and there were only a couple of hotel rooms available because so many of us were living in the house.

The other problem was, and it was a big problem: the A38 Chudleigh bypass road was now complete. So the large volume of traffic that used to go through Chudleigh – now didn't.

All those potential customers now just cruised down the new A38 dual carriageway and were oblivious to the fact that little old Chudleigh even existed.

It's sad – but basically true.

I guess with hindsight Mum and Dad should have thought about this before they moved, but I suspect they were like rabbits caught in the glare of a wonderful new working life away from the office work in London, life as a housewife, the hideous new M23 at the end of the garden and big planes flying over every few minutes (some even crashing).

But around that September time something happened that was even worse than the Chudleigh bypass being built.

We woke up to find out that Auntie Marjorie and Susan had left!

It was a big shock for us kids – but especially for Mum and Dad.

That was the end of sharing the burden of financial responsibility together.

Who knows what happened? I think Marjorie realised it was all too much for her and probably with Susan about to go to university, the decision to leave was made.

Well it left Mum and Dad in a boat without a paddle!

1974

Gran was also getting older and Mum needed more help in the kitchen. A local lady called Mary came and worked for us. She was a vital help for Mum and Dad and I think she was also a friend for Mum. It was good having Mary around and I would often hear Mum and her laugh together.

I have seen one of her children Jo a couple of times in the last few years and she told me that her Mum died quite a while ago. I'm surprised by how emotional that makes me, as I write.

Mary was a solid anchor in the storm of Mum and Dad's life at that time. Bless her.

Life at school was ticking along. I had made a couple of friends, David who also lived in Chudleigh and John who lived in Kingsteignton. It was good to have a couple of good-hearted friends. David was very good at football and other sports but he was happy to hang out with the likes of John and myself!

My favourite subject at school was woodwork and my favourite teacher ever was Mr. Farrant the woodwork teacher. He would keep classes in order but was also fun too if there was respect in the room.

It was around this time on Sports Day (yearly event) that I ended up winning the high jump out of all the people in my year. The bar wobbled on my last jump but didn't fall off, so I jumped the highest height. The sports day had different teams and I was part of the 'Raleigh' team so my win helped the team get more points. It's nice being popular! And on that day – I was.

Back at the Hotel – Mum and Dad asked if I would like to be the waiter in the restaurant helping Dad and they would also pay me per hour. I enjoyed waiting at the tables and helping out in the kitchen and getting paid. I was fourteen and it was a privilege to get involved.

I also started doing a morning paper round before I caught the bus to school. I had to get up quite early, walk down to Garretts the Newsagent, sort the papers into the correct order for delivery and set off with the big canvas bag full of papers and slowly unload them to the right houses. I had to walk to the outer edge of the town down by the A38 and back up the big hill again. But the good thing was, now the bag was empty!

In the winter it was a chore to get up early with the cold and rain but it must have developed commitment and character in me.

That daily discipline was to stand me in good stead for the long daily treks I was going to have to make in a few years' time when a similar commitment was needed!

But doing that paper round was also enjoyable and gave me a sense of achievement each day when I had completed it. I was also more alive and awake for the school day too.

My parents used to go to the local parish church in Chudleigh on Sundays. And we usually had to drag along with them. I was in Pathfinders a small youth group in the church and sometimes the vicar and his helpers would take us in his blue Bedford minibus on camping weekends. I used to enjoy these because the kids in Pathfinders were good kids and safe to be around. I have good memories of those times away.

But there was another camping week that I went on that had a totally different flavour. I was also now doing an after-school paper round that was a breeze compared to the morning one. On this round was a house in our road where a Christian family lived. I think they were part of a Baptist church somewhere. Anyway I used to sometimes on my paper round have a quick game of football in their garden with the two boys who were in the family. They were a bit younger than me and nice kids. Well one day they asked me if I would like to go on a youth camping week at a place called Rora House just off the A38 about five miles away on the edge of Dartmoor. I asked my parents and they agreed. So a few weeks later in the Summer Holidays I went to this camp. I suppose there were about sixty kids there camping in big ridge tents. The boys in my tent were good guys, all about my age apart from the one in charge who was sixteen. It looked like fun, playing football and other sports and all eating together at meal times. And it was fun... until... the evening meetings up at the house!

It was a sort of church service that we all had to go to. There was a talk and songs and praying and then a call to the front where kids would go if they wanted to give their lives to Jesus.

Well these evenings were quite emotional it seemed for a lot of the boys. Each night more and more kids were crying quite loudly as they went to the front. Now this was all too much for me. I was thinking this is scary and got me into a state of fear and the thought that this must be the devil at work.

And there were a couple of other boys in my tent who were also worried because word was getting around that by the end of the week everyone will be in tears at the front.

Well late one night about three days into this camping week I found myself awake in the early hours and I was not feeling well. So I turned on my little transistor radio and put my headphones into my ears so that the music would be some form of company and distraction. It was a long night and I was grateful for the variety of music that cropped up from the radio.

The next day I was still not feeling so well but I went up to the house to have a shower. And when I was having a shower, I noticed that my whole skin was covered in red spots.

After the shower I went and told one of the adults in charge of the event and when he saw the spots he arranged for my parents to come and pick me up and take me home. It turned out that I had got chicken pox, so that was the end of the camping week for me. And I can tell you, I was extremely pleased that I had chicken pox because I could now escape this crazy event and the prospect that I was going to be induced into a crying wreck and lose my sanity if not something worse by the end of the week!

A few of the guys in my tent were also worried about the evening meetings. I bet they wish they could have had chicken pox. I never saw them again to find out what happened. Pity… they were nice kids!

1975

Around this year I started getting into fishing. I would put my rod, reel, floats, lead weights, hooks and bait (usually worms or bread) onto my push bike and cycle to a pond or river. The River Teign was just down in the valley from Chudleigh and plenty of trout were in there although it was illegal to fish in it without a permit – which I didn't have! This didn't stop me though and I would spend hours hiding away out in the country by the river believing I was going to catch a big amazing trout. I never did though… but there was one day that could have been one of the best days of my life. I was fishing way out in the country by this deep and still bit of river with another guy. It was always a bit scary because there was always a possibility that someone would find us breaking the law.

One particular day we were at this amazing spot I had found a few days before which was behind some gravel piles and this very big trout would occasionally jump out of the water and land with a huge splash. It was the place to be!

A bit later my float went under the water – I had a bite! And the float stayed under meaning the fish was hooked. I struck the rod and felt the fish. It was big. Very big. Much bigger than any other fish I had felt. I started reeling it in and we could see

41

it as I pulled at it from the other side of the river. I was so, so, so excited. I didn't have a landing net because I wasn't as professional as that (but I wish I had had one that day!). So I asked the guy with me, who was a fair bit older than me, to step in the water and grab the fish, which was by this time right by the edge of our river bank in water only about a foot deep. He didn't want to get wet, although he was also as excited as me about the size of the fish. And before we had time to think – the fish got off the hook and escaped back into the middle of the river somewhere.

That was a day to forget. But I can never forget it.

The other fishing adventures I got up to were usually in the ponds that belonged to the Newton Abbot Angling Club. One of my favourite ones was called Tip Top, it was a pond on the road from Chudleigh. It has totally gone now (filled in by the nearby Clay Company that owned the land). The main ponds of the club were called Rackerhayes and there were a few of them in the fields opposite the Newton Abbot Racecourse. They are still used today by anglers.

I caught a 2lb. tench in one of those ponds and it was the best day of all my fishing adventures. I would love to tell you all about it but I think I'd better move on because too many fishing stories could bore some people. But that particular day made me so happy. I will always love that day!

I was actually getting quite busy those days with hobbies and social events. I had flirted with a few sports that I enjoyed playing. I joined a badminton club that met in the Chudleigh Town Hall once a week. It was my favourite sport and I was one of the youngest at the time which was fine. They would also meet up for social events too and I felt very much part of it all. It was good to be around more mature people who enjoyed being together on a regular basis. It was my favourite night of the week. I also ended up going out with one of the girls there for a few weeks. But I was a shy sort of guy when it came to relationships with girls.

Another sport which I enjoyed was tennis. I joined the Newton Abbot Tennis club for a year and used to play tennis with my friend David mostly. We also found an unused tennis court in a garden in Chudleigh and the owners let us play there occasionally. We played table tennis quite a bit too.

In fact David and I used to hang out a lot in those mid-teen years. We joined the Chudleigh Constitutional Club. We joined their skittle club league and both David and I were good. We joined the team run by the local sweet shop owner and we won the league once, and our team got a plaque each. David and I also won a darts trophy together. We were the youngest in the whole Constitutional club but people seemed to accept us. Many nights we went there and played snooker with our mutual friend Steve who also went to the same school as us and lived in Chudleigh. Steve was good at darts. He used to get a bit addicted to the gambling slot machines there. Mind you, David and I used to get a bit addicted to horse race betting sometimes. We would go to a little betting shop in Newton Abbot when we were out shopping for snazzy clothes on Saturdays. We never really spent that much though. We didn't have enough money to lose.

But I think David spends some of his days in those same betting shops even now.

It was David who introduced to me a musical artist I had never heard of before. But I ended up buying some LPs myself because I loved the music. The music was by a man called Rick Wakeman. He was the keyboard player for a group called 'Yes' and then he went off and did his own stuff.

Another album that I bought about the same sort of time was 'Night at the Opera' by 'Queen'. I ended up getting all their albums after that, whenever they released one. I even joined their fan club.

Talking of music, I had started going to local discos and loved dancing. (Still do!) The first time I ever let go with dancing was at a youth club disco in Kingsteignton. I just closed my eyes and let my body go with the music. It was quite brave of me really because at the time I didn't know that many people and there were older kids there, but after that it was never quite as daunting. I got freed up to dance pretty early in life so I have danced most places I have been over the years, even on the streets if there is good music playing. And I don't need alcohol to do it either, which is a bonus.

It was in 1975 that I was confirmed. Confirmation is a follow up to child Baptism.

I had been baptised, or christened, as a baby by my parents because they felt that it was the right thing to do. I of course didn't have much say in it all because I was a baby!

But now I did have the choice to confirm their decision because I was of that age where I could choose.

So this choice was given to me by the church Pathfinder group that I had been involved with. You may remember me telling you we used to go on some camping trips together sometimes and had fun when we did. Also on the times that I was taken to the church, Pathfinders used to meet up during the service in the house next door.

Now I can't really say that I particularly wanted to get confirmed. It's just that it seemed that I was supposed to. And there was not enough reason for me to go against it!

So I joined the other teenagers in the group and the Bishop of Exeter came to Chudleigh church and he carried out the service of confirmation. And I didn't run away, so in effect I was confirming the faith that my parents had baptised me into as a baby.

But that was about as far as it went with me. I hadn't had an encounter with God. And to be honest I needed one if I was to get excited about all this.

The only experience that I had encountered that had got my attention was the weird one at the camping week where those kids were crying. And that had made me want to get out of the place. And fortunately I got an exit door called chicken pox.

I was now at the age where life was getting interesting and church was not part of it. It was extremely boring actually and I was at the age where my parents were not going to force me to go to church on Sundays. So that was about it. I didn't bother going any more. I had too many other fun things to do.

I can't remember exactly what those other fun things to do were on Sunday mornings – but you get the idea!

Probably hanging out with friends or going fishing.

My sister Julie was starting to have boyfriends. She was quite popular and was always going out with someone. She was also hanging out in our next-door neighbour's house. There was a couple there called Wendy and Chuck. And Wendy would let Julie come round whenever she wanted. Julie felt more at home there than with us. Her and Mum used to argue a lot. Mum had different values to Julie. Julie was now thirteen and wanted to be free of how Mum expected her to live. It was a tough time and never really ever got better. Julie was into boys and hanging out on the streets with the Chudleigh crew.

I also hung out down town but not as much as Julie. I felt a bit more allegiance to Mum and Dad. But Julie and I still got on together fine. She used to stick up for me if people gave me hassle. In Chudleigh some of the youth called me 'pretty woman' which wasn't so good. It was because I had long hair and looked a bit girlish because of it. But it was refreshing for me to grow my hair because up till then Mum and Dad had always taken me to the barbers for short back and sides. And because of that, I was never keen on short hair. So this was my season for change. I got mistaken for a girl a few times in those mid-teen years, but that was the price to pay. Once I could grow a moustache I would be out of the woods!

I did have a few girlfriends around this time, often girls that I would bump into in Newton Abbot on Saturdays from other schools. I can think of three or four that I went out with. They would usually chat me up rather than the other way round because I was not so familiar with the dating scene. But they would get bored with me after a few weeks because I wouldn't kiss them. I didn't kiss them because I didn't know how to kiss. I had never done it before and was scared stiff of doing it wrong.

And... they were nice-looking girls. I fancied them, but I kept hitting the kissing wall!

1976

I was now in my last year of school. And the last six months or so were the best times I ever had at school. Now that I was in the top year (5th year, or year eleven as it is called nowadays)

46

there were no older kids above us, so that gave me a good feeling. Also some of the teachers were more like friends because some of us were more mature these days. And in the last few months some of the boys from our year were off the scene for some reason so there were less of us about. I think some kids didn't bother coming in much because they knew they would fail their end of school CSE exams.

I still loved woodwork best. Mr. Farrant told me that the objects I had put forward for the exam were the best in the whole year. I had made a coffee table, a small upholstered bench, a fruit bowl, a boat lampstand, a large sewing kit box, a chess board and some other items that I forget now.

 I was also enjoying building up a portfolio for my Art exam. But the subject I ended up getting the best grade for was History.

It is strange when you totally finish school. All of a sudden many of those people you have seen over the years each week are no longer in your life. They have all gone their separate ways and you don't see many of them ever again.

But this was the day I wanted over ten years ago after my first day at school. I had done my time! Now I was free to do whatever I wanted.

As it happens my Mum and Dad had another idea which entailed another year of full time education.

The nearest thing that I could think of as a career at that time was being a chef! I can't actually remember why though, but I would need some 'O' levels before I could start on that road and I had only taken CSE exams at school so far.

I could study for 'O' levels at the South Devon Technical College in Torquay, which was about fifteen miles away from

Chudleigh. That didn't start until September and it was still only May. So I was free for a bit!

Soon after I left school, a job advert came up in the paper that caught my eye. A pottery workshop was to start up in Chudleigh and they were interviewing for a team of staff. It was a sought-after job. I was nearly sixteen now and I ended up getting a position as a trainee pottery worker in the 'Wilson and Purdy' Pottery.

I was basically the youngest person on staff. About ten of us worked there and I was given various jobs about the place. It was sometimes hot in the building due to the two kilns they had. All the equipment was new because the whole venture in Chudleigh was new.

It was good to earn some proper money and I ended up saving quite a bit. I had always liked saving money and then buying something I really wanted, rather than spending it as soon as I got it. It was enjoyable to me to see how much I could save up.

Life back at 'Orchard House Hotel' was ticking along, although too slowly for Mum and Dad's liking. There were a few local people who popped in to have a drink at the bar in the daytime. I remember a lovely elderly couple called Mr. and Mrs. Clark who lived a bit further down Old Exeter Street. They would come in most days and be served by Dad. He used to like them I think.

But there was not really enough trade to make ends meet most of the time. People still came in for meals in the evenings and sometimes it was busy, but it was not consistent.

Gran had died in her sleep around this time so that was a shock for me. She was the first person I knew well who had died.

Julie and I used to watch TV together sometimes in the evenings in the upstairs lounge and there were no tight rules for bedtime any more since Mum and Dad had taken on Hotel ownership life. They were otherwise occupied downstairs in the kitchen and restaurant.

At the end of August I handed in my notice at the Pottery and told the foreman that I was due to start College the following week. He wasn't too pleased because he had expected me to stay at the Pottery for a long time.

With the money I had saved I bought a second-hand Gilera 50cc moped. The first time I rode it in Chudleigh car park, loads of the local youth were watching me. They used to hang around outside the Town Hall. I was so excited at having motor powered transport of my own. I let the clutch out and launched off with the engine revving 'high' and loving every bit of it. When I returned to the group of local youths they were all laughing, some with their ears covered. It was then that one of the older ones (who was going out with Julie) who had a motorbike of his own, showed me how to change gear. So there were more gears than one! It in fact had four! So then it was even more exciting.

I was now independent, I had my own motorised transport. I couldn't believe how good it felt, to just go off exploring anywhere and everywhere. And that's what I did at every opportunity I could get.

Having a moped revolutionised my life. It broadened it, inspired it and filled it. Those days of venturing off and exploring the distant lanes, villages, towns and landscapes were some of the best in my life. It was all so new, like being a child all over again, but without the restraints of other people's decision making. I could make my own choices whether to go left or right in the newly discovered lanes beyond the boundaries of

Chudleigh. Going round new corners I had never been round before. Seeing totally new landscapes of beauty I never knew existed.

No one knew where I was on those adventures. I was on my own. They were secret to me and me only. It was even better than daydreaming. I was free.

In September I started my new 'O' level course at Torquay Tech (Technical College). I remember that first day. It was not intimidating like school had always been. There was more of a sense of maturity about the place. The main building was like a small tower block (it has now all been demolished and a housing estate is there instead), it had seven levels, and was a prominent landmark in Torquay. My lessons were on level five. The College library was below on level four and on the first day of term I stood on my own by a big window on the fifth level and as I looked out below I was struck with the thought that I was entering a whole new period in my life. I was growing up and life was getting bigger and I was getting braver.

I occasionally rode my moped to College but most of the time I got a lift in from Chudleigh by a woman whose daughter also went to the College. She had a small green Mini Clubman car.

Most of my daydreams now were about going off on my moped exploring. I couldn't wait to get home at the end of the day and go off on my moped somewhere.

And as for the weekends! Loved them.

I was taking five 'O' level subjects, they were English, Maths, Geography, Environmental Studies and Economic History.

I was about the youngest person in my classes and many of the students were a year or two older than me, some even adults. I was quite mature, but not that mature and it showed up quite often in class. I was a bit of a joker. I liked getting laughs. It felt affirming. It was probably also a mask to cover my insecurity. I was quite inquisitive too, so if I didn't understand something I was not scared to ask. Sometimes I put my hand up, sometimes I didn't! Which annoyed the teachers if it was a silly question, which sometimes occurred so that I could get a laugh. A few times I was sent out of the class because of my distractive silliness.

There were also a couple of other jokers, so I wasn't the only one. I think we played off each other. It must have been annoying for those who wanted to learn. But generally the lessons went fairly well. I was totally lost with what was being taught in English, it was above my head. But I enjoyed Economic History and the teacher, Hugh Bodey had written his own book on the subject and it had been published. All the students had to buy a copy as it was the book we went through during the year. So he was on a winner!

I remember going off at weekends to places like the Sticklepath Forge on Dartmoor and the Morwellham quay museum, west of Tavistock on my moped to see the type of water wheels that we were studying. Any excuse to go exploring, but I did find the subject interesting too.

Also I quite liked Environmental Studies with Mr. Pearson. I remember studying different types of lichen and going off on my moped at weekends in search of them all.

1977

I was still at this time hanging out with David and Steve, playing snooker, skittles and darts at the Chudleigh Constitutional Club. We were in a local skittle league team, the three of us were quite good and often hit strikes.

I was also still in the Badminton club up at the town hall on Tuesday nights, which I enjoyed. I was getting better and more skilled with my shots too. A man called Graham ran the club, he was laid back and was always laughing. It was a good gathering of people. I enjoyed those nights.

David also had a moped, a Suzuki AP 50, so we would sometimes go off together to the odd disco in Newton Abbot. Then one evening at the 'Dyron's Centre Disco' a guy came up to us outside the venue with his mate. They were both older than us and this guy started grabbing us and accusing us of looking at him. We were both scared I think. I know I was. It all happened quite quickly, David broke loose from the guys grasp and the guy turned on me, somehow bent me over and kicked me in the mouth. My front teeth were both broken and there was blood. The guy must have been content that he had done his damage and we were allowed to get on our mopeds and get away from the scene. We rode up to the multi-storey car park and surveyed the damage. My teeth were smashed. I was very upset. It's hard to write how upset I was. Fighting was not in my nature at all. We rode our mopeds back to Chudleigh and I went home. Julie was there with her older boyfriend who was quite tough. Also Mum and Dad were there. I was really upset and crying, as was my Mum. Julie was really angry and wanted to get the guy. She was only fourteen years old, but the fact that she wanted to stand up for me was touching; bless her. The boyfriend said that he would find out about the guy!

We did find out a few days later that he was one of the toughest guys in Newton Abbot and was into fighting. My dad made me report the incident to the police and a few months later we were told that the guy had been in trouble with the police before for this type of thing. He ended up getting a caution on his record.

There was a big strong guy who lived in Chudleigh at the time, probably around the age of 40. He used to like me and when he heard about what had happened, he apparently took it upon himself to go into Newton Abbot to the place where the guy worked and pushed him up against a wall threatening that if he ever tried to do any harm to me ever again he would regret it.

It didn't get my teeth back, but it was the gesture I was pleased to hear about.

I had to get two front teeth crowns at the dentist – which costs money. They were a good match. But that night left quite a scar in me.

There were bully boys around all over the place. I was to bump into a few during the time I lived in Chudleigh. But we would soon be on the move again. Orchard House Hotel was not getting enough trade!

My parents were looking at properties in other parts of Devon.

Although for the time being we were still at the hotel.

In July I hit 17 years old. My college course was coming to an end and I passed my 'O' levels, but I didn't want to be a chef anymore. I had thought about being an Interior Designer, but it seemed a lot of work, which left the only real thing that interested me at that time. I wanted to learn how to fix my moped. And now I was 17 I hoped to buy a bigger bike in the near future. So… being a mechanic seemed the most appropriate career to explore.

My parents were looking at a property near Okehampton, next to an army base on the moors. It was a remote sort of place and the detached bungalow was not made of bricks, it was made of corrugated iron. It was called 'The Spinney'.

So while my parents put in an offer for the place, I looked through the 'Auto Garages' section of the phone directory. I phoned one called 'Wadman and Son' that was listed as being in the Okehampton area of Devon. The owner answered and I asked him if he had any jobs for a trainee mechanic.

He invited me to come and see him to have a chat. So I rode my moped from Chudleigh, through Bovey Tracey, through Moretonhampstead and further on down the road to Whiddon Down, which was where I found what I thought was the garage. But speaking to the man in the garage I found out that 'Wadman and Son', were a bit more off the beaten track. Near the village of Throwleigh, next to the 'Northmore Arms' pub.

So I got on my moped again and rode off towards Throwleigh. The garage was on a remote hillside surrounded by fields and in the distance looking south I could see Castle Drogo.

The owner was a character. Proper Devon! His name was Lionel Wadman. He was in his fifties and had apparently had a stroke a few years before which had slowed him down a bit and made him limp slightly, but he was still larger than life. His office was in a small caravan, next to a long outdoor breeze block ramp that was used to inspect underneath the small fleet of coaches he had. There were only about three coaches and they were used as school buses to take local kids from the surrounding area into the secondary school that was in Okehampton. Lionel's wife Pam was one of the bus drivers.

The garage itself was an old Dartmoor stone-built building and was joined onto the detached house that Lionel and Pam lived in. The yard, which was part field, was full of coaches, assorted Land Rovers, a horse transporter, trailers and cars.

On the small road outside was a little island with a tree on it acting as a roundabout junction. There was also an old red phone box and a red mail box. It was another world out there!

I told Lionel that I was living in Chudleigh but my parents were hoping to buy a house near Okehampton soon.

Well to cut a long story shorter, Lionel took me on as an apprentice mechanic. The apprenticeship would last 4 years and I would also go to Exeter College one day a week as part of the apprenticeship. I started in the September of that year. Each morning I rode my little Gilera moped the 25 miles from Chudleigh to Throwleigh. And obviously back again in the evening. It was a long trip each day but we were soon to live a lot closer.

The first day at work in the garage I was introduced to the two mechanics that worked there. Alan, who lived nearby in Chagford, was a friendly sort of guy and was in his early thirties. And Terry, who lived nearby in South Zeal, was about ten years older than me. They were both characters, as was nearly everyone who lived in that neck of the woods!

The first day I was there I was introduced to a tool that I had never seen before but that was soon to become a common companion, it was a ratchet. There was a lot for me to learn!

There were different types of spanner sizes depending on the age of the vehicles to be worked on. There was AF (the most common type at the time), Whitworth (which was for the older vehicles) and Metric (which was for the newer vehicles like

Renault and Peugeot). I was learning new things every day in a totally new environment and there was the whole issue of developing dexterity with my hands so that I would feel comfortable and agile as I worked on vehicles. And that is a skill that takes a long time to develop well.

The bike ride to work was fun and I was getting to know the landscape quite well after a couple of weeks.

I had started at Exeter College and that was a nice break for me and it was less far to travel from Chudleigh.

By about November I had decided that I needed a motor bike that had a bigger engine. The moped was struggling to do so many miles each day and it was slow too!

So Dad lent me a hundred pounds to buy a Suzuki TS 125 trail bike from 'Len Born Motorcycles' in Exeter. It had a few teething problems in the first week but eventually it was going fine and it was quicker to get to work and more fun.

Dad let me pay him back a set amount each week. He taught me the lesson that if money is ever borrowed from anyone, then any money you have is never your own until the full debt is paid back to the lender.

He was teaching me that responsibility comes with borrowing money, not to take the lender for granted and forget about the debt.

I have never forgotten that lesson. I paid him back in full as soon as I could. It took a while because I was getting less than £20 a week as an apprentice.

Soon after getting the Suzuki, I rode into Exeter College on the Friday which was my College day and one of the guys on my course came up to me as I arrived and said 'Your garage has burnt down'! He had heard that there was a big fire at 'Wadman and Son' and the whole garage had burnt down.

I didn't believe him at first, but it was true.

When I got home Dad told me to go up to the garage the next day and offer them any help they needed. I didn't work on Saturdays. But this was too important to ignore so I rode up there the next day.

The garage was gone. Just a burnt black shell was all that remained. There were quite a few local people there helping to clear up and sort through the mess to try and retrieve anything that was still usable.

Apparently Alan had been under a car in the pit and some petrol dropped onto his hand held inspection light bulb. The whole petrol tank was ignited and Alan only just managed to escape with his life. The whole place went up in minutes with a couple of cars in there too.

There was some humour, although stilted, as we searched through the mess. I had a dirty hat I used to wear at work and on the front I had sewn a little blue plastic Michelin Man. Terry said to me that when the fire was raging away, he had seen that little Michelin Man running as fast as he could out of the fire and off up into the hills. Terry said to me, 'You're not going to see him again!'

That stirred up some laughter, but all in all, it was a solemn day.

As it turned out, the garage kept running, but without any proper cover. There was one little wooden shelter that half covered a vehicle. The rest were worked on in the open. It was coming up to December and it was getting cold up there in North Dartmoor. Very cold!

The end of the year came round and it was Christmas. And all I wanted for 'this' Christmas was… me two front teeth.

1978

Well I didn't get the two front teeth back. But what I did get around this time was an amount of money that came to me after my gran's death. It was a hundred pounds or so I seem to remember. With it I bought a 1968 British motorbike that was in boxes of bits in the loft of a big house on the outskirts of Exeter. It was a 500cc Triumph Daytona. There was a unique feature about this bike that caught my attention. The petrol tank and both side panels (one being the oil tank) had been totally chromed.

It was going to be a project to get it back on the road, but the start of the project was buying it!

Dad helped me transport it all in his Cortina up to Throwleigh where Lionel allowed me to put it in the back of an old horse lorry that was parked up in the garage yard. That would be my personal little workshop to assemble the bike back together.

It was good of Lionel to allow me to do that, but I think he was quite proud of me riding fifty miles every day on a motorbike to work. And it wasn't always an easy trip.

That winter was particularly bad on North Dartmoor. It was very cold as was every winter up there, but this one had the added hazard of snow drifts! One morning I came to the last half mile stretch to work, (it was up a steep hill to a small hamlet called 'Providence') and was confronted with a massive snow drift right across the lane. And under the drift, just showing, was an abandoned JCB digger vehicle that had failed to move the drift and had itself become stuck and then had been covered by more snow!

There was nothing to do but attempt to go over the top of it all with my Suzuki trail bike. I got nearly to the top and then the bike started sinking a bit and I could not get it any further forward. I tried and I got hot in the process – and believe me, I had been very cold when I first reached the drift!

So I abandoned my bike on the top of this drift and walked the rest of the way to the garage. Alan and Terry laughed when I got there and told them where my bike was, but even they recognised the severity of that winter.

So yeah, I think Lionel was quite proud of me in some ways.

The new garage building project was under way in the yard but would not be ready to work in until after the winter. That was a bitter winter, working outside a lot of the time. My hands used to get so cold I couldn't hold the tools properly. And after riding twenty-five miles to work in that sort of weather I was already cold before I even started work. But Lionel and his family used to have me in the house to warm up. Lionel and Pam had one son and three daughters. Their son Michael was the oldest and a few years older than me. He was a nice guy but had no real interest in the garage trade really, but the company was called 'Wadman and Son' nevertheless. Their daughters Diana, Caroline and Teresa were all living at the house. Diana was a bit older than me, Caroline and Teresa were a bit younger.

They were a fun family and were often laughing.

My parents were still trying hard to get out of Chudleigh and the hotel business but were dealt an unfortunate blow when the sale of the house they hoped to buy near Okehampton fell through. So my long trip to work was going to have to continue for a while longer yet, it seemed.

At the end of January I passed my full motorbike test in Newton Abbot. I was now allowed to ride any size motorbike I wanted.

So I was now set up to ride the Triumph bike... when it was ready! I hadn't done much to it as yet because the only free time I got was after my work day shift and it was too cold and dark to work on it in the horse lorry at that time of year.

Lionel always wanted me to get my car licence. He used to take me out on breakdowns in the Land Rover he owned that had a small crane on the back. He let me drive it with L plates and he would be the passenger. It was a big tank of a thing, but I got the hang of it. I remember one night we went to a bad road accident on the old A38 out in the countryside somewhere. The police used to phone Lionel often when there was an accident or breakdown so that he could remove it from the scene.

Well this one night we drove to the scene of the accident and it was – a 'scene'! Blue flashing lights from police, ambulance and fire service vehicles. A pale blue Range Rover was all smashed up and there was a man trapped inside. It was a dramatic situation and the firemen were using all sorts of cutting equipment to try and get the guy out, but he was trapped quite badly so they had to be careful. There was the sound of a cutting machine and the taste of burning cut metal in the air, and to make matters worse the driver had big tins of blue paint in the back of the Range Rover, and the inside reeked of wet paint.

In the end they got the man out and rushed him to hospital. Then Lionel and I hitched up the Range Rover onto our Land Rover crane and took it back to the garage. That vehicle was in the yard for ages. I still remember that paint colour even now.

Anyway when I took my driving test later that year I failed. I had to turn off a main road into a small road on the right of me, the road was at the brow of a hill in Newton Abbot and just as I turned a car came speeding up from the opposite direction. I got across the road OK, but it was judged to be too close for comfort!

That small road on the right was shut off a few years later by the Council, because it was a danger spot.

I ended up not retaking my test and got into motorbikes in a big way from then on. If I had passed my driving test that day, maybe this story would have been very different?

But life was not all about failure. Early that year I ended up going out with a girl I had seen now and then on Saturdays in Newton Abbot. I fancied her but had never actually met her and didn't know anything about her.

Then one evening when I was hanging around down in Chudleigh town centre outside the Town Hall with the local youth, one of the girls said to me that someone she knew in Newton Abbot really fancied me. I asked her who it was and she explained this particular girl that I used to wave at from my motorbike in Newton Abbot on Saturdays. It was the one I fancied. I couldn't believe it. I was so excited!

She told me the girl's name was Suzette and then explained to me exactly where Suzette lived and the next day I rode my motorbike to Newton Abbot. I found the address and with fear and trembling, but also excitement, knocked at the door.

Well Suzette was in and soon after that we began meeting up. I usually went to her house. She was sixteen and her family were great fun. She was in a big family and we used to have a right laugh. And she was the first person I ever kissed on the lips and it was not as bad as I had feared. In fact it was easy... easy...!

Then some news came to me from my parents, they had seen a house they liked. But this time they were not going to buy. Now they had decided to rent. The house that they felt was the right one, was not near Okehampton. In fact it was not even on Dartmoor. It was nearer to the sea! About a mile away from the sea in South Devon to be precise. It was behind a church in Chelston, Torquay.

Well this put the cat amongst the pigeons! Instead of shortening my journey to work each day, it was going to lengthen it by ten miles. If I was going to stay at 'Wadman and Son' and continue my apprenticeship, I was now going to have to ride sixty miles a day. Crazy!

I thought maybe the move would fall through. A buyer for 'Orchard House Hotel' still had to be found, so nothing was set in concrete yet.

My bike trips to work each day brought some nice surprises on occasions. Foxes, for example, and once a vixen with cubs in line behind her

Another time I was about a mile from reaching the garage one morning (just down the bottom of the hill from where the snow drift was) and in the lane was a fresh dead badger. I say fresh because it looked like it had been hit by a car very recently.

When I got to work I told Alan and Terry that I had just seen a dead badger in the lane. And they said, 'You'd better be careful when you go home tonight because other badgers will come and collect it at some point and bury it and if you are there when they are dragging it off, they will attack you, and if they grab you they will never let you go because their jaws and teeth lock together.'

Alan and Terry were always joking about like that!

As I rode home that evening, the thought of that dead badger came to me and I did actually wonder if Alan and Terry may have been telling the truth. So I rode around the corner slowly with my headlights on full beam.

And guess what?

There were a couple of badgers dragging that dead badger along the lane. The lane was very narrow with high banks of earth and hedge either side. So I stayed well back from them ready to turn the bike around if they did decide to start running towards me. But they kept pulling it up the hill till there was an exit off the lane into a field. I waited till they were out of sight and then went as fast as I dared to go so that I could get out of there as quick as possible. I didn't want any teeth and jaws locking into my legs!

My love life was ticking along and Suzette and I went to a couple of discos at the 'Dyron's Centre', where my teeth had been kicked. I was a bit scared to go but with Suzette I felt braver.

The first time I went there with her we had a great night as it turned out, because Simon Bates the 'Radio 1 DJ' called me onto the stage and chatted with me and gave me a couple of 7-inch single vinyls as a gift.

I say my love life was ticking along, but in reality that is all it was doing. I, for some reason, took it for granted and would not see Suzette for a whole week sometimes. It was also hard because of my long days at work. But then I missed a weekend. So that meant I hadn't seen her for two weeks. My logic for leaving it for two weeks was that she would miss me more and we would be even more pleased to see each other when we did meet up.

This became a regular pattern in close relationships with girlfriends, that I would start to shut off after a couple of months into the dating.

Maybe that old rejection wound (from when I was a baby) was getting troubled. Too scared of intimacy. Didn't want my heart rejected.

Anyway, a day or so after I met up with Suzette (after that two week gap), she sent me a letter. She didn't want to carry on the relationship. We had only been together for about three months I guess, but I hurt deep down inside, and felt rubbish.

I could have gone and tried to make her change her mind I suppose but that would open me up for another dose of rejection and I wasn't strong enough for that. My emotions were already well over the edge of the cliff by now.

Very soon after that our family ended up moving to Torquay. The Hotel had sold and the house for rent that I mentioned before was still available, so the five of us all moved into the new home behind a church in Chelston.

I was pleased to leave Chudleigh in the end. It was quite an inward looking place back then. Nowadays it is a lot bigger due to extensive house building projects over the years. But back then, there wasn't a lot going on. Bit like living in a fishbowl!

And my parents must have been relieved to have got that financial burden off their backs. They had lost most of their money I think, hence the reason for renting.

My 18th birthday came around in July and I spent it with a couple of my friends who were on the same mechanics course at Exeter College. We ended up at a disco for adults on a council estate in Exeter. We got a bit drunk I'm sure. It was a strange place to celebrate my first night as an adult. If that's what I was?!

Soon after my 18th birthday my Triumph was nearly ready for the road. One of Julie's boyfriend's called Larry had helped me do the bike's wiring in the back of the horse lorry. He had a 750cc Triumph Bonneville and was good with Triumph electrics. It was good of him to come up to Throwleigh and get that sorted.

Over the warmer Spring season I had been able to get the rest of the bike together. The bike had literally been totally stripped. It was just a bare frame. No forks, no wheels, no engine, no nothing! All of the stuff was in boxes, so it was a good introduction to understanding where everything went.

So, by the end of July the bike was all assembled. Lionel suggested that I take it to the house of a local chap who lived fairly nearby. His name was Fred and he was in his late forties. He was an expert with bikes and knew about old British bikes like my Triumph.

Fred agreed to help me start up the engine and check everything was running well.

He was such a great help and I really needed it at that time, as there was so much I didn't know about the mechanical workings of a motorbike like the Triumph Daytona.

Back in Torquay my social life was now mostly involved with bikers. There were a few bikers in Newton Abbot that I hung around with, then there was a group called the 'United Bikers' that I also got to know, mainly because Julie had gone out with one of them earlier. There was the famous 'Marine Tavern' bar down by Torquay harbour that was only for bikers. It was run by a guy called Max and his sister Mon. It was a real grimy bikers pub that was famous all around England in its day, and there were always loads of motorbikes outside. People would travel for miles to drink there.

Julie again was the main link to the people who hung out there as she was going out with various bikers, not at the same time of course!

She was friends with Max and Mon behind the bar, even though they were quite a bit older than us.

I was nearly ready to have my Triumph on the road and was excited about showing it off to the biking fraternity in the area. I knew it was going to attract attention because of its unique chrome petrol tank, oil tank and side panel.

Then I would be a proper biker, with a proper bike. My hair was long, I had a black leather jacket and I was wearing dirty clothes. That was my basic membership into the scene at that time.

There was a craze amongst some bikers to sew black leather off-cuts, or patches, onto a pair of 'originals' (denim jeans). The jeans then became leather trousers in effect, once they were completely covered with the black leather patches.

These off-cuts were bought from a leather shop in Paignton. The hard bit was sewing them all onto the jeans. To be honest, my Mum did most of that on my originals. Bless her!

Then came the day that the Triumph was ready for the road. It was on a Saturday around August time.

What a day that was. I can still remember the smell of the heated engine as it ran for a few minutes in Fred's garden workshop. Then I rode it off to Newton Abbot. I was on the road and it was thrilling. The sound, the smell, the added exhilaration of speed and power that was now available and the whole sense of newness, the newness of a bigger experience in life.

That was such a special day.

I reached Newton Abbot and some biker mates were walking through town. When they heard the roar of a British bike in the street, they looked around to see what bike it was and who was on it.

And it was Mark Wadie, on a shiny chrome 500cc Triumph Daytona!

There were a few teething problems for a week or two, as there is with any new bike after a rebuild, but with Fred teaching me what to do, it all got sorted. From then on it was a life of polishing! Many a Saturday morning I would spend two or three hours polishing the aluminium engine covers and various other parts of the bike until they were spotless. Then I would ride into town or wherever and show it off.

The trouble was, it took a lot of polishing each weekend because it got pretty dirty and stained after a full week of riding up to Throwleigh and back.

One good thing was that I had managed to transfer my college venue once a week to Torquay College. So that saved me riding to Exeter. I could now just walk up the road to college. And that was definitely a bonus!

In my first year at Exeter College I passed both my main exams with 'Distinctions', so I was then offered a place on the 'Motor Vehicle Technicians' course for the next three years

In September, I started the 2nd year of my apprenticeship, now attending Torquay College once a week.

The house we were living in was behind St. Peter's church, and called 'St Peter's House'. It was a 4-bedroomed house and my parents paid £20 a week rent. So it was a good deal, even back then. We all had a bedroom each which was good. I remember I had a few big posters of Freddie Mercury and 'Queen' on the walls. My Mum used to say that every time she went in the room, 'That strange man follows me with his eyes'. I also used to listen to one particular track by the German Rock band, 'Scorpions', called 'Speedy's coming'. It used to rev me up and give me confidence before I left the house to go to the pub.

Julie was into the band 'Meatloaf'. She used to play the track 'Bat out of Hell' to death. Excuse the pun! She had a job in a Torquay shop down by the harbour printing T-shirts with a choice of colourful designs. She printed one for me with 'Triumph' on it.

Robert was also in a room of his own. He was now ten years old and went to the local primary school nearby to our house.

Dad had got a job at the 'Palace Hotel', as a gardener. The hotel had some nice grounds and even a small golf course. It was a step down from his past occupations but he was now in his fifties and I think he was pleased to have a non-stressful and easy life outside. He had always enjoyed gardening when we were living in Surrey, so it was something he liked doing.

At my work the new garage building had been completed in the summer. It was much larger than before the fire. It now had a long inspection pit with pit jack rails. The coaches could drive in as it was high and long enough to allow us to work underneath the coaches as well as the cars.

There were also plenty of racks for the storage of parts. There was a workbench area, an office and an important addition to the business was an MOT area with its own pit, rolling road (for checking brake efficiency) and headlight alignment rails and equipment. So this new addition brought in extra trade for Lionel.

The fire had probably been a blessing in disguise. The new setup was modern, roomy and a much better place to work in. Definitely better than working outside for another winter.

I had decided to continue with the apprenticeship at 'Wadman and Son', after we moved to Torquay. It was further again to travel but I was learning a lot of things and it was a pleasant environment in which to work. My boss and colleagues were good people.

My daily duties were changing as I was given more responsibility. I was making up metal brake pipes to replace rusty or damaged ones. This needed the use of a flaring tool that I was getting the hang of; relining brake shoes with new asbestos linings with the use of brass rivets; decoking cylinder heads and grinding in the valves; fitting clutches; servicing; removing tyres with a hammer and levers, and mending punctures in either the tyre or the tube; stripping carburettors and inspecting them; replacing various bushes and bearings and adjusting the applicable components afterwards.

There were still many things to learn, but slowly I was picking up new skills on a variety of different vehicles including coaches, lorries, tractors, trailers, motorbikes and of course cars.

There were a rich variety of cars too. Old heavy Rover saloon cars, Triumph Heralds, Renault 4's, Morris 1000s, Reliant three-wheelers, Land Rovers, Ford Granadas, Mini's, Jaguar Sovereigns, Austin Allegros and many other choice specimens.

As the year came near to its end an event was to occur that brought about a change to the biker world in South Devon.

The event was – the closing of the 'Marine Tavern'.

Bikers could no longer meet there anymore. The building was going to be sold.

It was the end of an era.

1979

Julie was now going out with a guy called Vern. He was a few years older than me and owned a Triumph Bonneville. It had murals sprayed on the tank that he had done himself. Skulls, women, dragons, that sort of thing!

Well Vern was a sprayer and was used by some of the bikers whenever they needed their bikes sprayed. I was never going to get my Daytona sprayed – I was very happy with the chrome tank!

But that was Julie's current boyfriend. And Vern knew quite a few of the bikers that hung out at the old 'Marine Tavern'. A large number of ex-Tavern bikers now needed somewhere else to meet.

And one of the places they went was the 'Noah's Ark' in Paignton. It was there that I started meeting a new crew of bikers. They decided to start a club and wear brown leather arm patches (made by a biker who worked with leather called Friar) with the name 'Taverners' on it.

I ended up joining the club. It was sort of run by a guy called Malcolm. He was a friendly chap and had a big Yamaha 1100. He was married to Jules who was also very friendly. After a while the club hung out at another pub called 'The Globe' in Paignton and that became the regular place to go. At weekends I often used to sleep at Malc and Jules house which was just up the road from 'The Globe'. Another biker called Magg who was also in the 'Taverners' became a good friend and we used to spend a lot of time together. We used to hang out at Malc's, and stay up all night chatting and drinking till daylight the next morning. Jules was a late bird as well. There was always some sort of party going on after the pub closed and we were right on board with it all. We had this pair of thin black leather gloves and we cut the fingers off. I wore the left one and Magg wore the right one when we were at the pub or out and about and not on our bikes.

There were about twenty-five of us 'Taverners', including some of the guys' partners. Magg and I were sometimes known as brothers because of the glove thing. That was the reason we wore them in the first place, to symbolise brotherhood.

We were slightly younger than most of the others in the club. But we were well up there with them?! Another couple in the club were called Tony and Marion. They were both older than

71

us and also lived in Paignton. Tony had a Triumph Bonneville and worked in his Dad's bakery nearby. He used to work a night shift and made all the bread and produce for the bakery in the early hours. Magg and I would often turn up at Tony's bakery and sit around the big warm ovens chatting together with Tony as he rushed about doing his bread stuff!

There were also a couple of girls (Val and Elaine) who were about our age and used to hang out with Magg and I at Tony and Marion's house chatting and listening to music through the night. We weren't going out together, but we used to enjoy each other's company and usually met up at the weekends.

I used to long for the weekends. They were my favourite part of the week by far. College was on a Friday too which was good because I could get home before it was too late, get myself ready, listen to the Scorpions track(!) and get off to 'The Globe' to be with my best friends.

As a club we would sometimes go off to a biker rally somewhere. A rally was a place where a few hundred dirty bikers got together in some field, drank booze, ate burgers or suchlike, listened to live Rock bands, looked around at each other's bikes, camped in tents and sometimes we got a metal badge to pin to our leather jacket that had the name of the rally on it.

Well Malc and a few others in the club came up with the idea to organise our own 'Taverners' Rally in South Devon somewhere.

Our rally would be called the 'Shytehawk Rally' referring to the local seagulls, because in South Devon you get a lot of them, and often their s--t falls from the sky!

We set a weekend in Spring, the following year (1980), for the first 'Shytehawk Rally'.

We would all have our different tasks to get it organised. It was going to be done well. People from all around the country would come. And that was in the days before any internet or mobile phones.

In the summer, Julie, her boyfriend Vern and myself went away on our bikes for a couple of weeks.

We took our tents and sleeping bags on the back of our two bikes (My Daytona and Vern's Bonneville). We set off from a biker camping weekend we had been to, called the 'Devon rally', which was held near Braunton in North Devon each summer. From there we headed east along the amazing cliff top coastline from Lynton to Minehead, with the Welsh hills in view to the left across the Bristol Channel. It was an exhilarating route. We then went over the Severn bridge to cross the Bristol channel. From Chepstow we rode North up through the River Wye valley and past the Tintern Abbey ruins. All of this scenery was beautiful and the road through there was so conducive to riding a motorbike. I was loving it. So were Julie and Vern.

We then passed through Hereford and on up through to Chester where we stopped for the night and stayed with some relatives of ours. Then the next day we carried on North to the Lake District and what a buzz that was. So much amazing scenery up there!

At one point we had to drive through a section of road near a farm and the whole road was covered in fresh wet cow pats. A herd of cows must have passed through that way just before we got there. Vern was in front so he went first very carefully...

but not carefully enough! He started slipping sideways and before long they came off.

They weren't hurt... but they were messy. They were laughing after a few seconds and got the bike upright again and pushed it on through to clean tarmac. I went very carefully through after that and didn't fall off. But I didn't have Julie as a pillion (passenger). And that made the difference, I am pleased to say!!

We carried on till Carlisle and spent a few days up there and around the Lake District. Then we travelled back South to the Long Marston disused airstrip near Stratford upon Avon. The 'Three Spires Rally' was being held that weekend and there were hundreds of bikers camping. It was a well-known rally at the time. There were 'Outlaw' gangs there like 'Hells Angels', 'Chosen Few' and some others I forget the names of now. 'Outlaw' biker gangs wear colours (their club patch) on their back. They were a lot heavier league than us. They were a law unto themselves and carried an intimidating atmosphere around with them.

This particular rally was run by them. There were bikes charging up and down this airstrip at some crazy speeds. One guy was on this new Honda 1000cc bike that had just come out in the shops. He was completely naked and went screaming up this airstrip.

I can't remember if it was him or not, but around the same time someone came off and crashed badly at speed. An ambulance turned up and took him off. He was in a very bad way. Whether he lived or not I'm not sure.

It was good being with Julie and Vern. We knew a guy called Stryder and he knew quite a few of the heavy guys in the gangs, so we hung around him. There was one incident in the big tent one night when we were sat in a circle on the ground together when this dodgy-looking character who was in one of the 'Outlaw' gangs came and sat down with us... after slamming his own personal axe into the middle of the circle and into the earth.

So there was plenty of heavy vibes around the place.

After the rally we went and stayed at Stryder's house for a night or two.

From there Julie and Vern set off back to Devon, but I had an extra week so I rode off in a South East direction by myself and headed to East Anglia. My mum's sister Margaret and her husband Paul and their family lived over by the coast near Cromer. I went and stayed with them for a couple of nights. It was good to catch up with my cousins again. We hadn't seen so much of each other since we had moved from Surrey to Devon.

From there I decided to go to Horley and see my old haunts.

I went and stayed with my friend Steven from Horley school, the one I mentioned I used to lend my bicycle to at lunchtimes. His parents and his sisters were pleased to have me turn up on their doorstep and were lovely hosts to me.

I went to see my old house (Ellerton) on the outskirts of the Town. The owners let me walk about and reminisce.

The bough coming out from the old sycamore tree, which dad had hung the rope swing from all those years ago was still there. The rope swing was long gone, but the tell-tale scars left on the bough were still very evident for someone such as myself to ponder on.

The busy M23 was now very much a part of the scenery. And the planes were indeed more frequent.

It was good we moved.

During my stay in Horley I decided to go and face my 'old demons'.

I went round to the house of the guy who used to bully me. He had grown bigger, like I had. All through my school years I was one of the shorter pupils in whatever year I happened to be in, but after I left school I put on a growth spurt and ended up over 6 foot tall! Which is always useful now and then.

I ended up going out to some big 'Rockabilly' type disco near London with him and another guy (called Robert) who used to be in our class. I got a bit drunk and did a lot of dancing even though I was a bit out of place with my long hair and dirty biker apparel. I told you I liked dancing! Even at a 'Rockabilly' event.

The other two were rummaging around the place looking for someone to fight I think. I just got on with my drinking and my dancing.

On the way back to Horley that night Robert, who was drunker than me, lost control of the motorbike he was riding and went off the road and through a hedge. He was smashed up a bit but managed to get back on his bike and get home. When the three of us got back to his place we could see that the accident had cut his face quite badly. He would have a scar for sure, even after all the blood was cleaned up.

I stayed around in Horley for a couple more days looking around and meeting people. It was on this visit that I was told Simon Gallup (our old classmate) had just joined 'The Cure', as their bass player.

When I left Horley that week, the last person that said bye to me was old bully boy. I camped the last night in his parents garden. He had been pleased to see me and in one way I was pleased to have seen him again, but for a different reason. I was pleased to have faced my old enemy. Now I felt empowered.

I think he was still a bully at heart and at the end of the day I wouldn't have wanted to hang around with him for too long, but the visit did make me realise that it was a good job my parents left Horley when they did. Because if they hadn't, I am pretty sure my life would have turned into more of a hell hole than it was back then. I would have been led along a whole different path. And the 'real' me, would have got buried.

In 1979 I almost lost my license. I had been done for speeding once (like 36mph in a 30mph zone). Also a couple of years before on my moped I had had an incident occur that got me an endorsement.

Anyway it put two endorsements on my license. And if you got three, you were banned!

Then one night coming back from work at the end of the week I got stopped by the Police, claiming I was speeding. They had only just started following me, but that was the situation I was in. They gave me a ticket. I reached home sat down for supper with my parents and my young brother and burst out crying. I couldn't believe it. I was going to be banned for a year now. My job would end and so would my passion in life: riding my Triumph and being a biker. It was too much to take in.

I went to 'The Globe' that night in a very solemn and downcast state.

My dad ended up privately writing a letter to the Devon Superintendent of Police, asking that they might find it in their heart to let me off this one time, explaining my committed effort in riding to Throwleigh on my bike each day to ensure getting my apprenticeship completed and that without the use of my motorbike, my job would end.

A couple of months later I was about to walk to the College for my study day and there was a letter from the Police. They had decided because of dad's letter to totally let me off.

I was so flaming amazingly happy that day when I went to College. I had just bought some black leather biker boots that I really liked and was wearing them for the first time and then the crazy letter from the Police. I was floating on air! What a day. And then it got better again. Loads better!

A really attractive biker girl at College who I had secretly fancied for weeks, came up to me out of the blue and started chatting to me. We had never talked before. Well it seemed we both fancied each other! So that night I took her to 'The Globe' on my Triumph and I introduced my new girlfriend to my biker friends.

That was some day!

During the year I had a couple of girlfriends, but they were short-lived as usual. I was no great lover it seemed.

As autumn started setting in, a few of us from the 'Taverners' were off to a biker bar over near Axminster (on the coast) in East Devon.

We were approaching Exeter on the small stretch of road called 'Peamore bends'. It was called 'Peamore bends' because it was right next to a mansion house called 'Peamore House' and at that particular place there was a long S bend in the road. As we approached 'Peamore bends' we were going quite fast, so I shut the throttle down a bit and then throttled it up again as I started to bank into the first left-hand bend. There was a huge bang from the engine and as the revs died away, I thought, 'What on earth has happened?' I was going at such speed that I just dipped the clutch and freewheeled the bike up and out of the bends. The momentum slowed and I finally came to a stop by a little monument just past the gate and driveway to 'Peamore House'. It was in that very house that I had bought the Triumph from a guy called Patrick a couple of years before! The bike, as I mentioned before, had been in boxes in the loft of 'Peamore House'.

Well as I looked down, there was a big HOLE in the front left-hand side of the engine. All my oil was in a long line back along the road I had come from and as I walked back down the road I found a mangled con-rod bust in half. It was my con-rod and it belonged inside my engine, not on the road!

It was a huge downer for me. The other guys carried on to Axminster, while I waited for an AA vehicle to pick me and my Triumph up and go back to Torquay.

I got the Triumph dropped to my house and got a lift from there to 'The Globe' pub in Paignton where other guys and girls from the 'Taverners' were drinking at the bar. I explained what had happened to my engine. One other major concern apart from how I was going to afford to rebuild it was, how would I get to work each day!

Then after an hour or so, Tony and Marion came up to me and offered me full use of Marion's bike until I got mine fixed. Marion had a Honda XL 125 trail bike. It was a real special gesture by them. Her bike was quite new and would be very suitable for the trip each day, especially in snow, which did occur again that winter.

I have always been grateful for Tony and Marion's kindness in lending me their bike at that very difficult time.

Another strange coincidence in all of this, was that about twenty years after that day, Marion was a passenger in a fast car at that exact same place, when a tractor pulled out in front of the car causing an accident in which Marion died.

Marion was a lovely person and so is Tony. Their support for me in lending that Honda, I will never forget. It basically helped me keep my job, because there was no other way of getting to work.

I ended up going to London on the back of Gary's Norton Commando. Gary was in the 'Taverners'. He had to go to London for something, so I got a lift with him to go in search of some second-hand aluminium engine cases for my Daytona. I managed to get some for my model from a bike-breakers, which was a real achievement. I also got some replacement conrods and new stretch bolts for the big ends. I would get my old crankshaft ground and buy some new shell bearings and pistons when I got home.

Gary was a keen rock guitarist and was in a local band. His favourite band at the time was 'Wishbone Ash'. And that night as we were riding back from London with me carrying all my engine stuff on the back, Gary says to me, '"Wishbone Ash" are playing in Taunton tonight, let's go and see if we can get tickets.'

So we went to the Taunton Odeon, but the concert was sold out. Gary said 'Wishbone Ash' were his favourite band and that we had come all the way from London on the Norton to see them. Well the door staff went and talked to the band's road crew and they came out to see us. They opened a back door and led us up some stairs to the band's dressing room, where they showed us to leave all our bike gear, including my engine! Then they took us into the auditorium where 'Wishbone Ash' had already started their gig. Gary was in his element. And after the gig. Guess what? We ended up being led back to the dressing room to get all our stuff and to meet the band. We all chatted for a while and they were interested to hear the story of how we got there, and Gary talked about guitar stuff. He was definitely in his element now... chatting to 'Wishbone Ash' in their dressing room. Match made in heaven!

After a few weeks I got my old Triumph going again and it went better than ever before! The reason that it threw a rod out the front of the engine was this: as I removed the sludge screw from the crank I found that the oil way through the crank that feeds the big ends was all blocked up with hard sludge. It was hard to get it all out, but in the end I did. It had been the left-hand side big end journal that had been struggling because it was further away from the oil pump (which is on the right-hand side of the engine). So it had seized on that journal and had then thrown the rod out of the engine and into the road!

It was very good to be back on the road with my beloved Daytona.

1980

For most of this year I didn't wash my hair. I washed it at the end of last year, but didn't wash it again until September. It was part of a friendly bet with one of the guys in the 'Taverners', to beat his record! Only difference was, I was a mechanic – often underneath dirty vehicles. But a man's gotta do what a man's got to do. I was a dirty biker after all.

I used to wear a plaited leather headband at work to keep the hair out of my eyes, but it didn't do the same sort of job as my old hat and Michelin Man that got burnt up in the garage fire. That hat would have been useful in this anti-washing season!

It was another hard winter at the beginning of this year. There was black ice on the roads in the early morning. And black ice is treacherous, especially on a motorbike.

The journey from Torquay to Newton Abbot was not so bad because it was a busier road and that part of South Devon is protected from the bitter North East winds by the hills of Dartmoor. Also the milder salty sea air keeps the roads near the coast a bit safer, but once I started getting past Newton Abbot towards Bovey Tracey and the edge of the moors, the roads got more slippery. Once I was the other side of Bovey, on the road past Lustleigh, to Moretonhampstead, it definitely was stress time for me. Black Ice. Not normal ice. Black ice is in another league.

After Moretonhampstead there was less traffic as the road proceeded to Whiddon Down. As the journey went on it grew even colder. Then off the main road and onto the remote lanes that wind their way to the garage on the moors. I was out in the wild. Those roads were too tricky for a car, with that sort of ice around.

I fell off my bike a few times, I can tell you. And it hurt, as well as scratching my pride and my bike. So those winters were hard to endure.

I had to stop sometimes three or four times on some of those winter journeys because my hands would get soooo cold. Especially my thumbs. It literally nearly broke me some days. I wanted to give the whole thing up and stop this stupid apprenticeship.

It was only my Dad that stopped me packing it all in and I'm glad he did.

He used to say to me, 'Mark, I know it's hard for you, but just stick with it, the spring is nearly here and it will get easier. It's only a couple more years and then you won't have to do it anymore. And you will be a fully trained mechanic and that will help you, all through your life.'

I'm crying as I write this. My beautiful Dad did some good things for me as I was growing up.

I will tell you what I had to wear each day to try and stay warm (and dry). Two pairs of socks; one pair were big thick woollen ones. Big leather biker boots, or Wellington boots if it was raining. Then I wore jeans with my overalls on over the top of them, then thick waxed canvas biker leggings over them. My torso had loads of layers including a very thick sheepskin waistcoat that my Dad used to wear in the Second World War when he was at sea with the Merchant Navy. It was a necessity for me to wear that. Even when I did wear it underneath my coat, I still got cold and wet sometimes.

On my head I wore a balaclava, my helmet, a scarf covering my face and a perspex visor clamped onto my open-faced helmet to protect me some more from the icy wind. But often that would mist up so I had to remove it.

Then... on my hands... I would wear thin silk gloves, thin wool gloves, leather gloves, then waxed cotton biker mittens over those three pairs. And I still ain't finished! I bought some waxed cotton handlebar accessories that went over my handlebar grips and acted as wind protectors for the hands to slip inside of but still enable the rider to operate the throttle, front brake and clutch.

And do you know what? It still wasn't enough. I used to have to stop a few times each morning to jump up and down to help my feet get some warmth into them; then put my hands on the engine for as long as I dare and run about (if it was not too slippery) to get my body warmer. I actually felt physically sick some mornings when I stopped by the road because of the cold. Then a few miles down the road, I would have to stop and do it all over again.

I would take well over an hour sometimes getting to work, but Lionel understood when I was late. They used to let me go in the house by the stove and get warm, before I could start work. Oh the pain in my thumbs as they thawed out was the final part of the whole episode. I'm glad I don't have to do that anymore!

The spring of 1980 did arrive, eventually! And with it came the excitement for us 'Taverners' of running our own rally. The 'Shytehawk Rally' was nearly upon us!

A farmer who owned some fields just outside Newton Abbot had agreed for us to rent one of his fields. He knew it was going to be noisy, but was up for it and he was going to be paid for the inconvenience!

Some rock bands had been booked. The headlining act was going to be a band called 'Breaker' from Exmouth.

A marquee was booked, a welcome tent was booked, a bar with plenty of booze had been organised, food was arranged – including a pig spit roast; light blue metal badges had been made, tickets were printed, adverts in biker magazines had been placed – the main one being 'Motorcycle News' – and the police had been informed.

Well the weekend of the rally arrived and we were there ready at the field with everything in place to start welcoming bikers from around the country to the first 'Shytehawk Rally'. Importantly the weather was good.

Bikers started arriving, paying for their ticket at the welcome tent, and then riding their bikes to the area of field where they put their tents up. They then started mingling with everyone: drinking, eating and soaking up the atmosphere.

It was happening!

Gary and Larry and another couple of club members working at the welcome desk were smoking joints and getting well stoned. It all helped the friendly atmosphere when people arrived for the weekend. The welcome tent was evolving into the drug tent!

Quite a lot of people arrived on the Friday night and by midday Saturday there were a few hundred bikers that had come through the gate.

A big tug of war tournament was organised and different biker groups created teams. We had our 'Taverners' team that Magg and I were both in and it was during the tug of war that my filthy originals (worn out jeans) which were over my leather patchwork trousers, fell to bits. I hadn't washed them in over two years. They were oily, ripped and smelly. But that was how bikers were back then. It was all part of the deal. Nowadays it is 'all-in-one leathers', very clean, very colourful, very expensive. That wasn't our world back then!

My originals had to die at some point – the cotton was rotten!

And the 1980 'Shytehawk Rally' was their graveyard and date of death. They had been a good friend.

We won the tug of war though...

The rock bands started playing later in the day and by the evening it was party time. People were getting drunk and stoned and things were going well. At the end of the night 'Breaker' started playing and went down a storm. People loved their music. They wrote their own songs and Val, Julie and I decided to have them do a gig at our combined birthday party later in the summer at a pub in Torquay.

The next day people slowly started going back to their homes and we were left to clear up the mess, but there were a lot of us, so it was fun.

The rally ended up making a profit for the club. So the money was put away for another possible 'Shytehawk Rally' the following year.

Not long after the 'Shytehawk Rally', Magg and I got chatting about stuff. Both of us were getting bored with the rather laid back approach of the 'Taverners' social life. The rally had been really good, but generally people in the club were not up for venturing out of Torbay as a club much, not even just going off for adventures after the pubs shut at 11pm. People often just went off back to their homes. Magg and I always wanted to stay up really late into the night and hang out with 'life'. We didn't wait all week for the weekend to arrive to just have a tinker about and then go bed!

A lot of the 'Taverner' crew were a few years older than us and some were settling down with partners and stuff.

But we didn't want to 'settle' down! We wanted to be up and about, rubbing shoulders with other people who didn't want to settle down. We wanted to be in a club that were riding the roads as a visible group on a regular basis, exploring new territory together and staying up through the nights at weekends... grabbing as much time as possible.

I was keen to start a new club of our own and I put the idea to Magg late one night at Gary's house after a party. Everyone else had gone to bed.

I mentioned a name that I thought would be good for the club and Magg was up for it. The next thing was to chat about who would join the club, apart from just Magg and me!

We both toyed with the idea of four slightly younger guys whom we had recently met. We had chatted to them at the 'Shytehawk Rally' and they seemed a bit like us.

We agreed that we would ask them as soon as possible. The name of our club if they said yes, would be 'Mephistopheles'.

It was the name I had seen ten years before on the bicycle frame of Kevin's (our Horley neighbour) brother. You may remember I mentioned before in the book. I had been told by Kevin, that Mephistopheles was the messenger of the devil. And the name had obviously stuck in my memory somewhere, to unearth at a more appropriate time. Now was the time.

We very soon got together with Gordon, Jerry, Jon and Ross. We went off together one night on our bikes to a pub in Stoke Gabriel to broach the subject with them. On the way through Paignton, Jerry was going too fast and missed a corner and went straight across the centre road markings, amazingly missing the oncoming traffic. He went up onto the grass verge the other side of the road, scraped one tree, went the other side of another tree a few meters further on, then fell off and just missed going straight into a third tree.

We all stopped. As quick as we could get our act together, we got away from the scene before any police turned up. Jerry was only slightly hurt and his bike was quite bent, but he was able to bend offending items out of the way and ride it again!

I am telling you – Jerry nearly died that night. All six of us were amazed at how close he had been to hitting the oncoming traffic and the three very solid trees!

Jerry was the youngest in our group and was in fact not quite seventeen for a few more days, so he was not supposed to be out on his Kawasaki 250 Triple. It was a fast bike and he was not yet legal to ride it and his Dad did not know he was out on it!

Anyway, he came out the other side alive and unhurt and that was all that really mattered at the time.

We then carried on to the pub in Stoke Gabriel and after we got our drinks, Magg and I told them we wanted to start a club called 'Mephistopheles', and asked them whether they wanted to join.

Well they did – so that was that! We were rolling!

We used to meet up at the house of a guy called Paul around that time – a biker who was renting a house next to the old Audley Park Secondary School. We asked Paul if he would make some club arm patches for the six of us. We chose to have a large yellow Pentagon (which was seen to be a satanic symbol) sewn onto a round piece of brown cotton, with 'Mephistopheles' sewn around the top of the circle and 'Torbay' around the bottom of the circle. Inside the five points of the pentagon we used some strange spiritual letters that indicated each of our respective names. So each patch was very slightly different. In the middle of the pentagon were the letters MCC that stood for Motor Cycle Club.

We ditched using leather jackets and wore mainly black heavy duty work jackets which at the time were called 'Donkey Jackets'.

Me, Jerry and Gord

They were a statement of difference, to the conventional biker look. As time went on we mixed it up a bit with leather flying jackets, trench coats, camouflage jackets and occasionally even the old leather jacket, if it got too cold!

The day came when our patches were ready to sew on our jackets. We now had an emblem of belonging to each other and it felt good. We had crossed a line into a whole new adventure together. From now on we were knit together by a common bond of something akin to brotherhood, our bikes and our new club identity was the glue that knitted us together. Not sure if you can knit with glue? Let's call it poetic license.

Me with my beloved Daytona, *photo by Chris Chapman*

In August I went up to Derbyshire with Gary (the guitarist) to see a load of rock bands that were on the line up of 'Monsters of Rock' festival at Castle Donnington.

Gary wanted to go because the band 'Rainbow' were playing their last gig together (with their present line up).

The official attendance that weekend was supposed to be thirty-five thousand people, but other sources put it at sixty-five thousand and the suspicion is that the lower number was stated due to legal safety reasons.

There were a lot of people anyway!

Some of the other bands playing were Saxon, Judas Priest, Scorpions and Riot.

But the main headlining act was Rainbow. Ritchie Blackmore (Ex Deep Purple guitarist) was in the band at that time, as was Cozy Powell (the famous drummer), Roger Glover (Ex Deep Purple) and Graham Bonnet (lead singer).

As the evening came to an end there was a spectacular light show, with fireworks. The sky was full of colours.

Gary was again in his element, similar to the time we had gone to the 'Wishbone Ash' gig. He particularly respected the skills of Ritchie Blackmore and had sprayed the 'Rainbow' insignia on his Norton 850 Commando petrol tank because of this fact.

If I'm honest, I didn't get really excited by seeing all the bands. In a way it all seemed quite empty. Not really meeting the mark. Whatever the mark was! My name being Mark, is not the mark I am talking about here! But funnily enough, maybe that is the mark that I am talking about...

Over those years, before and after, I got to see a lot of big bands, but I always seemed to leave disappointed, with an undercurrent realisation of – well they aren't the answer... they didn't bring real satisfaction.

Here are some of the bands I got to see:

Buzzcocks (first proper band I saw live, in '76)
Siouxsie and the Banshees
Ultravox (with Midge Ure)
Hawkwind
Black Sabbath (Heaven and Hell Tour)
Motorhead
Thin Lizzy
Girlschool
New Order
Rick Wakeman
Rory Gallagher
Whitesnake
Screaming Lord Sutch
Simon and Garfunkel
Rainbow
Judas Priest
Saxon
Scorpions
And there will be others I have forgotten about I'm sure.

I even got to see the legendary 'Queen' live show in the Milton Keynes bowl (1982). My heroes from ten years before. Freddie Mercury, Brian May, John Deacon and Roger Taylor. I bought every vinyl album of theirs through the years, usually on the day each was released.

But even at that gig, I was secretly thinking, 'This isn't it'. They are not as important as I thought they were. It was still an empty experience for me. I had expected more. But the 'more' never got delivered.

The nearest thing that was getting delivered to me on a fairly regular basis, were my times with the 'Meps' (our short name for 'Mephistopheles').

As the months went on, we did more and more things together. There was one memorable occasion early on as a club when we got our faces masked up with face paints. Each of us had a fairly sinister painted face that resembled the sort of style that the American Rock band 'Kiss' used to paint their faces. (See the photo of me in white waistcoat on page 89.)

Each of our faces were different from each other but similar in style. Each of us were painted with totally white face paint and then various designs were put onto the white background. Red and black being two colours that featured quite a bit in the designs. There were also a couple of new guys about to join the club and they were with us that night.

Then we set off into the night on our bikes. We were going to a party organised by a friend called Philly. She was part of a group of bikers that used to meet together under the name of a group called 'The Y Society'. They were good friends of ours and we couldn't wait to turn up with all our newly painted face personas.

On the way there we roared down through the centre of Torquay, where loads of people were milling around outside pubs and nightclubs and various food joints.

Well, as people looked up at the roar of bikes coming down through town, they were shocked to see our faces. We were giving off a very intimidating presence with those faces on and we knew it. It made us feel unique and somehow important. Each one of us knew we looked shocking... and it was giving us a big buzz.

Word had also got out to the police that we were roaming around I think, but they didn't know where we were headed, so we didn't come across them till much later in the night.

We reached Philly's and all of us were happy to be together, each excitedly talking about our feelings of riding as a big group past the many onlookers.

We were in our element!

We left Philly's well after midnight and set off into the night through the country lanes. When we reached Paignton seafront we were all pulled over by two policemen in a police car. They overtook us and turned on their blue light and we all stopped our bikes behind them. We knew they were going to be shocked when they got out of their car to walk back towards us all and look up into our painted faces. And they were.

They didn't really have anything on us and had to eventually let us go on our way. We didn't really say much to them. We just stayed quiet and mysterious and only answered their questions with the basic information that was required from us.

We left the scene wearing confident smirks.

We ended up riding the bikes down the long steep road through some woods to Babbacombe beach. We were looking for somewhere to sleep. We managed to get into some old beach huts and that's where we kipped! It had been a good night.

When the sun rose on the far horizon of the sea, we emerged. As we trooped out of the various beach huts, someone was looking down on us from the beach café roof. He also got a shock, and didn't say a word. He was on his own and there were lot of us! It was another policeman.

Another big part of the camaraderie within the 'Meps' in those early days as a club, was fixing and improving our beloved bikes together.

One of the main venues for this sort of activity was in the garage of Ross's parents. Ross still lived with his parents, as we all did at that time. His Dad was great and let Ross and us guys work on our bikes into the night.

We always had something to do, to improve the cosmetic look. That suited our particular quirk of fancy. Often it would be things like higher ape hanger handlebars, thinner seat designs, smaller back lights, removal of indicators, dog leg levers, exhaust systems, sexy looking air filter boxes and a host of other assorted types of modification.

These times would also include important maintenance projects. Fixing oil leaks was a common one, because most of us had British bikes, that were prone to adopt oil leaks nearly every week. But there were also wiring faults, suspension problems, strange engine noises that used to concern us and force us to dig deep into the engine, sprockets and chains to change, loads of things that called for our attention. And if by any freak of nature the bike was running perfectly, we got the tube of Solvol Autosol out and cracked on with polishing the beautifully crafted aluminium engine cases and various bits of chrome that were only half shining and not really displaying their full potential.

Those bike maintenance times together as a group also bonded our friendships.

As a club we were meeting up with a mixture of other interesting characters in the biking scene away from our local haunts.

There was a time in December of this year when a bunch of us 'Meps' rode up to Minehead, on the north coast of Devon, to hang out with a big hairy biker called Des. He had a Honda 1000 Goldwing and he used to do tyre spinning doughnuts with it. It was a big heavy bike, but Des made it look small. We stayed with him for the weekend and got to meet his crew. It was good to get out of Torquay and the regular scene. We were to do it a lot more as the club continued to explore the unknown horizons outside of our little world.

It was also in December of this year, while I was at work, that across the air waves on Radio One came the news that John Lennon had been shot dead. It was startling news at the time. He had left the 'Beatles' long ago, but he was doing his own music with Yoko Ono. They had just released their new album 'Double Fantasy' the month before.

Now with this sudden death, the vague possibility of the Beatles doing a one-off gig in the future (with the original 'four'), was out of the question.

A few of us 'Meps' stayed up through the night at Ross's house and played 'Double Fantasy' a few times over, mixed with other John Lennon music, including old Beatle songs.

I suppose it was our 'Princess Di' moment. It's not something I would do now. But we were young and it felt right to do at the time. It was a memorable evening.

1981

This winter was not so hard on me, because a situation had arisen that enabled me to sleep in a house in Chagford over the week (at weekends I went back to Torquay). A lady from Chagford called Margaret was the part time secretary at the garage and she offered me a room in her house so that I would not have to travel the long distance on my bike each day in the winter.

It was a really good offer because Chagford was only a few miles from the garage, and she even cooked me supper every night and breakfast each morning. I think she only charged me two pounds a night, if anything at all.

Later in the year our bike club went up to the pub in Chagford, to see Margaret's son John, play in a Rock band. Then we all went to the garage in Throwleigh and Lionel let us all sleep in one of the buses parked in the yard.

I had entered the final year of my four-year apprenticeship. Alan and Terry were still the only other mechanics working at the garage and the three of us got on well enough. Lionel was still ruling the roost and the whole scene was a pleasant one to work in. I had learnt a lot since I started back in '77. There was still plenty to learn though.

All sorts of characters came to that garage. I can't even start to mention them, but quite a few of them were caught on camera by a well-known photographer that lived in Throwleigh. His name is Chris Chapman and as far as I know his books and photographs of Dartmoor life are still extremely popular. Most of his work is in black and white.

When I first worked up at Throwleigh he used to drive around in his little Reliant three-wheeler van and he brought it to us if it had problems.

He often caught on film the very same people that I used to meet in my everyday work, in that rural setting in North Dartmoor.

The 'Meps' had been slowly growing since the original six started up. The first few that joined in the early days were from around Torquay like Rob, Russ, Scott, Colin, but not all club members were from the area. There was Kim who rode British bikes and was from Kingsbridge. He was one of the early additions to the club and we used to hang out with him and other similar-minded bikers from his area. Kim used to try and make it down to Torquay for our weekly meetings though.

There were another couple of guys from Plymouth called Gruff and Si. They were good mates and often used to come and stay at weekends and go off to rallies around the country with us.

Then there was Greg, and Mitch (his girlfriend), from Clevedon, near Bristol. Greg owned a BSA chop, customised with long forks. Greg and Mitch often used to come and hang out with us, and we also used to go up there to Clevedon and Bristol to spend the weekend with him and his crew. Greg was an actual member of the 'Meps' and wore the patch. Mitch didn't because only guys were members.

There were many different girlfriends that were in our crew for a 'while' and then were gone, so it would have been quite divisive and tricky for the club if they had been patch members, but they were very much a part of the fun we all used to have together.

There was one girl I must mention though and that is Dena.

Jerry and Dena got together fairly soon after the club started and Dena was a big part of the 'Meps' for a season. And there was many a time when a few of us used to sleep on the floor at Dena's place over the weekend. She used to be a good host to us. It was good to have a place where we could actually stay the night and relax together.

It was at Dena's one night when we were having a party getting drunk and stoned, that I got Scott to walk around in a circle in the kitchen with me chanting for the devil to come into us. Now I DEFINITELY don't recommend you do this, it's something I would never do again. But it is what we did on that particular night. And it got scary. Scott got scared and when people tried to get into the kitchen to stop it, they couldn't. The door was jammed shut.

Who knows what got into me that night. We were tapping into unknown forces without really knowing what we were doing. The very fact that we were wearing the Pentagon and identifying ourselves with 'Mephistopheles' didn't help. But that was where we were at.

Another house we used to gather at after work (in the early days of the club) before we went out for the evening was Gord's parents' house at the bottom of Shiphay Rd. His Mum Evelyn was lovely and made us drinks and even fed us.

We were always looking for pubs that would allow us to hang out as a bike club. They weren't easy to find but one of the pubs that we used to call our own was 'The Clarence' which used to be opposite Torre Railway Station. It was sort of our clubhouse for a while. It has since been demolished and there are flats there now, which is sad. Well, probably not for the people who live in the flats!

Another regular meet-up place and haunt was 'The Pullman' bar which was underneath the Grand Hotel, next to the main Torquay Railway Station. Likewise it is not in existence now. But the door that we used to enter by is still there. It hasn't been opened for years. Who knows what there is behind it now? There used to be a big long cellar-type bar.

It was in this year that my parents again moved house, but this time they stayed in the same town! They moved to a small terraced house in Cambridge Road, in the St. Marychurch district of Torquay.

Only my brother Robert and I went with them. The place was too small for all of us because it only had three bedrooms. Julie wanted to move out anyway. She and Mum had their difficulties. She moved into a flat with a mate called Paula and was working at a photo processing factory in Paignton.

Mum was working as a nurse at a big residential home. Dad was still working as a gardener at the Palace Hotel.

When the month of May came around, the second 'Shytehawk Rally' came around too. The 'Meps' went for the weekend of course, as it was in our neighbourhood. It was much the same as the year before. Only this time Magg and I weren't involved with all the organising, setting up and setting down. It was good to hang out with some of the old faces again, though to be honest we were always meeting up in this or that pub or party somewhere. The biking scene was very big in South Devon. Everyone was brushing shoulders here or there, or somewhere else.

In the late June, the bike club trooped off to Stonehenge. It was the summer solstice coming up, but the main reason we were going was because there was a bike rally in the fields nearby.

We met up with Greg and Mitch before we got there and all went in together.

There were quite a few 'Hells Angels' around so we didn't feel too relaxed, but we put our tents up and no great dramas kicked off.

On the day of the solstice, we went up the road to the Stonehenge site and when we arrived there were loads of people in and around the site as a Druid ceremony was being carried out by Druid priests dressed up in their strange garb for the occasion.

Some of the 'Meps' climbed up onto the big Stonehenge stones (illegal now) to get a good view point and to let people know we were there.

We noticed a guy with an expensive camera take our photo a few times and found out why the next day! Our club were on one of the pages of the 'Sunday Times' newspaper, stood around and sat on the stones, with an article written below it.

Magg still has the article to this day.

We went on so many trips to different concerts, rallies, parties, bike shows and the like. The weekends in particular always got us off doing something. We used to have a lot of fun.

But there were times also when it wasn't so nice. Sometimes we would fall out with each other, get jealous of each other and temporarily take sides. There were a few times when I would go off on my own and feel so lonely and upset.

It was a wake-up call that even my best friends were not always reliable.

There were other times when we were getting on and other people wanted to hurt us. But that was more in a physical way.

There were a few scuffles and fights between our club and other characters that wanted to stir up trouble. I personally never liked those times. There are people in this world that do like fighting and there were a few in our club who seemed to enjoy it.

But to be fair they never went looking for it, else I don't think I could have stayed in the club.

We were generally a nice group of guys that looked quite intimidating but underneath were far from it. It didn't take long for people to find that out once they talked with us.

In July I hit my 21st birthday.

In August, twelve of us went to France for two weeks on our bikes. It was a trip that started a whole new way of thinking for my life.

The weather was sunny and we all got red faces and arms. We went down through Brittany and hung around Saint-Jean-de-Monts, by the Atlantic coast, North of La Rochelle.

Me near the
west coast of
France

There were a few disagreements between some people but we all managed to stay as one group and agree in the end where we would go and where we would stay, because we had no schedule. And it was this very thing, along with being in a totally different country that got me excited about 'Life'.

The only other time I had been outside of the British mainland was when I was in the Scouts about ten years before and they had taken us camping to Guernsey for a couple of weeks.

This experience now though, was totally different. I remember going off for a walk on my own along a beach one morning in the sun and thinking, 'Wow, this is the first time in my life when I have been free to go left or right and make my own decisions away from home, school, work and all the other similar constrictors through growing up. This is the nearest I have been to experiencing "freedom".'

And I liked it. And I wanted to live that way a lot more. And I was getting a sense that it was possible. It was opening my eyes to an exciting future. I was feeling Alive.

I shared my thoughts with the club and asked if anybody was up for not going back to England and just staying out here.

You can see I was keen!

Well Scott said he might. But in the end, he backed out. I had Gord on the back of my bike; so he needed to be considered.

My time would have to wait. My apprenticeship was about to finish in a couple of weeks so it was wise that I returned to England to complete that anyway.

Back at work I wondered how I would broach the subject of leaving. But I didn't have to worry. Lionel had obviously realised that once I was classed as a skilled mechanic, he would have to pay me as such. For four years he had legally only needed to pay the low apprenticeship wages.

He had decided to let me go. So it was one of those situations that forced me into a new direction and actually it was the perfect solution that I needed to launch me towards my dream of travelling.

Lionel was good to me and gave me an extra couple of hundred pounds to give me a fresh start.

I went back for a week to rebuild a Triumph 650 engine for a chap that lived in Throwleigh. He had asked me if I was interested in rebuilding it and he would pay me for all the work done. So I said yes, because I needed to save some money to get me out of England to see the world.

It was proof that I had learnt a lot in those four years, because I was now very capable of stripping and rebuilding a motorbike engine. And that was the reason I had chosen to be a mechanic in the first place... to be able to fix my motorbike!

Those skills have gone on to help me in many other ways too.

My Dad had been right to encourage me to stick at it and finish my apprenticeship.

Soon after I left the garage, I was at home in Torquay and the phone rang. It was Lionel's wife Pam on the phone.

Lionel had died. They had been in Spain together on a short holiday. (It was rare for Lionel to go on a holiday.) Lionel had collapsed in the hotel with a heart attack. The body was being flown back to England and the funeral was to be in Throwleigh church, in a few days' time.

Well that was a big shock for everyone, me included. I rode my bike up to Throwleigh and the church was packed. Lionel was well known to a lot of people around North Dartmoor.

It was a sad day, especially for Lionel's family. Two of his daughters, Caroline and Teresa were still only teenagers at the time.

I have good memories of Lionel and my time working up there on Dartmoor. It was the start of making me into a man.

I had decided to cut my long hair off around this time. It was amazing how much more vision it gave me! No longer hanging around the sides of my eyes. I think I did it in preparation for going travelling.

I wanted to wander the world and be free to just move on to somewhere else whenever I wanted. To do that sort of travelling I first needed a fair amount of money to tap into when I needed it. And as yet I didn't have that sort of money.

Then one day I was going to Basingstoke in a lorry with Gary (the guitarist friend who I mentioned earlier). At the time he was working for his family's meat business and he was driving their lorry to pick up some meat. I went with him for the day.

He was also going out with my sister Julie at the time.

Anyway we were talking about my plans to go travelling the world. I mentioned that I was going to have to get a good amount of money before I got into it big time and he said, 'There's good money to be earned in Australia. Julie and I hope to get married in the new year and go and live there. That's the place to get yourself some cash.'

Well that was the spark that got me on a mission!

I would get a ticket to Australia, get a job there and save a load of money so that I could then go off wandering. And be free.

Good plan? Yeah good Plan!

First I needed to get enough money together to even afford an air ticket to reach Australia, because they weren't cheap.

But now I had a plan and a goal. I started up a bank account at Barclays Bank in St. Marychurch. I needed to put every pound I could into that account until I reached the air ticket price and it is amazing how fast that account got added to.

It was an enjoyable mission I was on, to save first one hundred pounds, then watch it reach two hundred and so on, always getting nearer to the bigger figure I needed, for the 'air ticket'.

1982

In the Autumn of '81 I had sold my beloved Triumph Daytona and bought a Kawasaki SR 650 custom bike.

The reason for getting rid of my British bike was mainly because the Triumph factory up near Coventry had collapsed. Japanese bikes were becoming more popular and the British bike trade was suffering.

A couple of years earlier a few of us with Triumphs from Torbay rode our bikes up to the big factory at Meriden, near Coventry, there we converged with literally hundreds of other Triumph riders on their bikes. From there everyone rode to London, where more bikers on Triumphs were waiting for us to arrive. A huge petition was handed to the government to appeal for their help in saving the Meriden factory from closure.

It was an amazing day, bikers from all over the country turned up. The government did put some money into it as a result I think, but it only saved it for a short time. The factory ceased production not too long afterwards.

As a result a company called Wassell started making pattern parts and the owner moved to Torquay and opened up a British parts shop, right in Paignton.

Well I had better not say too much, for obvious reasons, but many of us British bike riders suffered with all this pattern reproduction. Parts were not made to the same quality and when those parts are an integral part of the engine, it gets very depressing, especially when you've spent a lot of time and money on fitting them to your beloved pride and joy.

It was soul-destroying actually.

So the time came to go the easier and less hassle route.

The Kawasaki SR 650, had come out two or three years before and I always fancied the look of it. It had four cylinders and looked sexy to me with its mag wheels, the one at the back being smaller and fatter than usual, which lowered the back end; and it's 'prismic' custom tank, with slightly higher bars. I sold my Triumph for £700 and bought the 'Kwak' for less at £500.

Magg and Gord and Jon, still had their British Nortons but Jerry had owned a Kawasaki Custom 750 for most of the time in the club. Ross and a few of the others were already riding Jap stuff.

In addition to the Kawasaki I also owned another bike that I had obtained over a year before. Tony from the 'Taverners' and I had bought an old 1958 Triumph 650 pre-unit bike. We had both put in £100 each to buy it, but after I finished my apprenticeship I gave him the other £100 and became the sole owner.

I ended up going to Vern's workshop in Newton Abbot with the frame and cutting it near the headstock and Vern welded in some extension pieces of metal to extend the frame neck into what is known as a goose neck. It extends the whole length of the bike. I was going to make it into a customised 'Chop'.

Gord stood by my Kawasaki 650 and my Triumph 'Chop', nearly 9ft long

So 1982 had started and it was good to have had a winter where I wasn't having to ride to Throwleigh.

My days now were spent doing various jobs for people and earning money that was going straight into the bank. And I was doing well. I had got some work on the River Dart, helping to restore a couple of boats. I remember working down there one day and the new 'Queen' single with David Bowie getting its first air play on Radio 1. It was called 'Under Pressure'. I loved it and went out and bought the record on the spot. It was not long after this that I ended up going to see my beloved 'Queen' play live at the Milton Keynes bowl.

I got my Kawasaki sprayed black by Vern, with the Mephistopheles logo put on the side panels, added high handlebars, re-covered the seat, fitted chrome air filter boxes and basically got it looking the way I liked.

Gord was often round my house and we spent a lot of time together working on our bikes. I managed to get hold of some chrome ten-inch over-springers, which are basically long struts of metal with springs that you often see on chopper motorbikes (those who know – will know!).

I also got a six-inch bolt on extended hard tail, which does away with the conventional rear-framed suspension system. It lengthens the bike some more again, but it is an uncomfortable ride when going over bumps in the road! I got a guy named Johnny, who later joined the 'Meps', to make a uniquely shaped prismic petrol tank. It only ended up holding a gallon of petrol, but you win some, you lose some! I also got a nice sixteen-inch fat back wheel and tyre to match.

All this creativity ended up being handed over to someone else in the end.

I assembled it the point of being a rolling chassis and soon after, a friend called Lino, who was in the 'Taverners' and liked my style, offered to buy the bike. He gave me his Yamaha XS 650 bike and added some money with the deal. So now I had a Yamaha. My plan was to spruce it up a bit and sell it, to help me get the money to go to Australia. I got the tank and panels sprayed light purple and did some work on the rest of the bike and sold it to Philly who was looking for a bigger bike.

The Yamaha XS 650

By now I had enough money to buy the air ticket, so I bought a return ticket, to fly to Brisbane on August 20th.

There were a few months left before I would leave, but I had made the step. It was on!

In May, Julie and Gary got married down at Cockington church in Torquay. Julie was still only nineteen, but it seemed to be what she wanted. Our brother Robert was running around taking photos alongside the photographer. It was strange seeing all of us bikers dressed smartly in suits.

About this same time Magg's old girlfriend Sarah, who I had not particularly liked before, seemed to be extra charming and I fell for her. It was all quite surreal. I had a ticket to go and live out in Australia and now I seemed to have been slightly derailed!

We both seemed to have been caught up in an unexpected whirlwind love affair. We were happy and excited to be together and within a short period of time were working at getting Sarah enough money to also fly out with me.

We bought a cheap old BSA bantam and stripped it down together, painted it up, fixed it and sold it for twice the amount. We also went to autojumbles together and bought and sold a few things. We got the money together for her and she managed to get a ticket on the same flight as me on August 20th.

There was a lot of rushing about in those final weeks. Going around saying our goodbyes, going to parties and sorting out what things to take for a year... or longer if things changed!

August arrived. I managed to sell my Kawasaki for a good price a few days before take-off, so I had some money put away until things got a bit settled over there.

Val, who I mentioned earlier in the book, had got married to Steve. They were both ex-'Taverners' and had decided to go and try living in Australia for a while.

Sarah and I would be able to stay at their place for a couple of weeks until we found our own place to live.

Our leaving party was out at Cornworthy, in the countryside where Sarah's parents lived.

My Dad pulled me to one side and said privately, 'Mark don't feel you have got to come back after a year, stay out there and explore, the world is big, you are young, there is plenty to see.'

He was also letting me know that if he hadn't have got married to Mum and started a family, he would have loved to stay at sea and explore some more.

What a good Dad!

Well Sarah and I got to Heathrow and it was hectic. I saw Patrick Muir from 'Call my Bluff ', in amongst all the crowd! Pretty sure it was him.

I had never been on a plane before, so I had chosen quite a long journey for my first trip!

We stopped in Bangkok for a stopover and when Sarah and I got out of the plane the heat from the engines in the wing was really powerful. I couldn't wait to get down the steps and onto the tarmac and away from the plane. But when I reached the tarmac it wasn't any better, so I hurriedly walked away from the vicinity of the aircraft, that didn't help either. It was then that I realised, Thailand is hot... and humid!

Yeah, we sweated. We had a free room in the airport hotel because there was some delay in the flight. So we got a taxi into Bangkok and explored. Someone gave us each an orchid flower necklace and we didn't have to pay for them. Thai welcome gifts. Thanks Thailand!

Then the taxi driver took us down some back streets and we thought, 'Oh no, we are going to get robbed.'

But as it turned out he was taking us to a building in a seedy back street. Inside there were lots of women behind a glass panel, dressed only in colourful underwear. As the women started smiling at us, it became blatantly obvious what the deal was. This wasn't the place we wanted to be.

As I'm writing I have just thought of the animated movie 'Madagascar', where one of the characters who wants to get away from an awkward situation says to his friend, 'Just smile and wave'.

I think that's exactly what Sarah and I did... 'Just smile and wave'!

When we arrived in Australia, (I was 22 years old) it was a thrill for our senses. A whole new life experience for us. The temperature was warmer, the people were livelier and at the same time more laid back, the sky seemed bigger and brighter, and the houses and shops were different.

England seemed very distant now.

It was all very exciting. We stayed with our friends Steve and Val who were renting a house near the ocean's edge at Shorncliffe, north of Brisbane.

They showed us round the local area and acquainted us with some of the information that we would need to get a place of our own.

We stayed with them for a couple of weeks before finding a flat in a suburb called Windsor, which was closer to Brisbane city centre. It wasn't long before I managed to get a job at a local Holden (Australian make of car) garage. It was a posh garage that sold new cars. My main job was to carry out the pre-sale checks on the vehicles that were going out. I avoided telling them that I didn't have a car license, so when I went on the road to check everything was working, I made sure that I didn't go too far from the garage. I didn't want to come across the very diligent traffic police!

One day when I was working in the workshop, it started to rain really heavily. The most rain I had ever known. It was a deluge of water coming from the sky, which turned the roads into rivers. Manhole covers flew off as the pressure from underneath blew them into the air.

Then ten minutes later, the rain stopped and the sun came out, as if nothing had even happened. Apart from the missing manhole covers and the gradual disappearance of the newly formed rivers!

In October Julie and Gary arrived in Australia. They rented a flat also around Shorncliffe. It was good to have another couple of Pommies that we knew well from Torquay out in Brisbane with us, as well as Val's younger sister Sandra from Paignton who had come out later.

But it soon became evident Julie and Gary's marriage was not all a bed of roses.

While I was working at Leach Motors, I had bought a cheap second-hand four-cylinder Honda 500cc motorbike which was useful for exploring the city and getting me to work each day. Sarah had got a job in an Italian delicatessen and she worked with a lady called Kath, who was renting a house with her partner Rick, in a suburb of Brisbane called Morningside. After a couple of weeks they offered us a place in their house to share the rent with them, so we moved over to Morningside.

It would be honest to say that mine and Sarah's relationship was also not a bed of roses and we were to go our separate ways before the year was out.

In September, soon after we arrived in Australia, the work visa laws changed. You could now no longer renew a one-year work visa. I had entered the country on one, so early on I realised that my time in Australia would only be for a year. It was a bit disappointing, but also helped me on my mission to save money and wander the world. It may have been too easy to hang about in Australia for years on end if the law hadn't have changed. Then I would have got myself into the same rut of normality that I had been so intent of getting out of in the first place.

Also soon after my arrival in Brisbane, I had seen an advert for Australian Railways, they had vacancies for railway workers. I had gone for an interview but had heard nothing back from them.

By the end of the year I had again moved house. Rick, Kath and myself rented a big old wooden traditional Queensland house in a southern suburb called Annerley. I had also got a new job in a nearby bike garage called 'Ropart Honda' in Moorooka. The owner was an Australian guy called Gary and as well as fixing motorbikes, we also sold and fixed lawnmowers.

He and I used to listen to the cricket at that time because England were in Australia for the Ashes. (I had been to seen them play at the Gabba Cricket Ground when they were in Brisbane earlier in the year).

Sometimes after work we used to smoke pot together and get pretty stoned. One time when I started sensing I had floated to the top of the workshop, Gary looked up at me and said 'Mark come back down'!

I can't say I always enjoyed getting stoned, often I didn't. It was a mixture. A mixture that I kept exploring, and couldn't sort out.

The most common type of bikes I worked on at 'Ropart Honda' were little red Honda 110cc bikes that were used to deliver mail. We had a contract with the Postal Company to service and fix their bikes.

Working at 'Ropart' was OK, but the problem was, I wasn't earning a lot of money. Not enough money to save for wandering around the world after I left Australia.

The end of the year was upon us and unfortunately for me, Australia won the 'Ashes' and England didn't!

When you are a 'Pommie' in Australia and you lose any big sporting event to the Australians, especially cricket, and especially the 'Ashes', you aren't allowed to forget it!

On the last evening of 1982, Rick, Kath and myself went into the City centre to get in on the New Year celebrations. We went in fancy dress. I went as Alice Cooper, with all the black eye make-up. I had won a fancy dress prize in a nightclub a couple of years before in Torquay, dressed up as Alice Cooper. Back then I had had long hair and I looked the part.

The city was buzzing, people were getting drunk, and so were we. While wandering around half-drunk a big Maori guy hit me full in the face for giving his girlfriend a 'Happy New Year' kiss. I had never met either of them before. The hit put me flat on my back, but because his fist was so huge it must have been like a big cushion and my face was totally unhurt. There was no big drama. Apparently it is not an accepted Maori practice to kiss someone else's girlfriend. To be honest it's not that accepted outside of the Maori tradition either!

But I was drunk and that's one of the downfalls.

As the night went on, Rick and Kath left the centre and went back home to bed. They were about ten years older than me, so they had a bit of an excuse. I went into an all-night club.

1983

When the club was nearly empty, I decided it was time to go home. As I emerged onto the street, it was daylight! I wasn't expecting that.

So I set off in my bedraggled Alice Cooper attire, with equally messy black eye make-up, in the vague direction of home. It was going to be a few miles walk to get back to my house. I was tired and rather self-conscious as I walked along the now fairly busy main roads out of the city. It's one thing looking like I did in the night, when it's party time, but the morning after, when it's daylight, it's a totally different experience. I must have walked for about two hours. It was a long and lonely walk.

And I felt very much alone on that first day of 1983, in more ways than one.

As January rolled on, an unexpected letter arrived at my house. It had come via one of my previous addresses. It was from the Australian Railway Company. They were offering me a job as a railway porter at South Brisbane railway station. The job was to start in a few weeks' time if I still wanted it.

Well I did want it. It was going to be a lot better pay and it was going to be a whole new experience that looked like fun.

Before I left 'Ropart', I sold my Honda to one of the customers who was keen to buy it from me, and I bought a Yamaha XS 650 twin. It ended up being a decision I regretted. The Honda had been good and reliable transport. And the Yamaha ended up being a hassle.

In February I started my new job as a railway porter. South Brisbane railway station was set in a suburb of Brisbane that had a large aboriginal population. It also had a lot of alcohol problems. The station was the end of the line for the Interstate route from Sydney in New South Wales to Brisbane in Queensland. The trains that did this route had nine or ten sleeper carriages and also mail trucks for transporting all the Interstate mail. So the porters had to unload the mail and sort it, get the sleeper carriages cleaned and ready for the return trip to Sydney and keep the station clean and tidy.

It was basically quite a cushy job, that paid well and carried some good perks, such as reduced fares and even free travel, if you worked there for more than six months!

There was often time to just relax. I remember one of the porters called Wayne. We used to enjoy each other's company and would sometimes smoke a joint together. Once, it went to Wayne's head and he was spaced out and it was a juggling act to keep him out of the way of the station master. He was a good friend that I would have liked to spend a few more years with.

Me and Wayne socialising one evening

There were also a couple of born-again Christian guys who worked on the crew. One was a Welsh guy, called Dennis. He was nearly sixty years old and used to preach to me. I used to shun him off a bit when he did that, but he was a really nice chap and was like a father figure to me. And some of his God talking made sense. But I had no appetite whatsoever to become a Christian. If he needed a crutch, then that was up to him. But I certainly didn't.

The other guy was called Leon and he was from Sri Lanka. He ended up in hospital after he threw some petrol on a fire in his garden. The fire came back at him and burnt half his ear off. I went to the hospital to see how he was. He was very grateful for my concern and invited me to his family house for meals sometimes, where they often talked about God and the Bible. But I kept myself out of their reach. I had a world to discover and explore and I didn't want to think about God stuff. That would just get in the way!

The only spiritual stuff I was interested in at that time, was reading a book or two that some spiritualist guy had recommended me. They were by an author named Lobsang Rampa. He was writing about a spiritual dimension that was intriguing to me.

Maybe there was another dimension that couldn't be seen. If there was, then that was exciting and I wanted to know about it.

A few weeks before I left England I had gone to see a medium, to have my future told. I think a couple from the 'Taverners' had recommended this particular lady. Well she had caught my interest a bit when she said that she could see me wandering through a dry and dusty land on my own. At the time I had thought, well that's Australia. And that's where I'm off too.

I guess I was open to a spiritual dimension. But it wasn't going to have anything to do with boring Christianity.

While I was living in Australia, David Bowie was hitting the charts around the world with his new song 'Let's Dance'. He went to the outback of Australia to film the video for the song in a typical Aussie outback pub.

I didn't get to see him… but I did get to see two other famous people from the music scene when I was out there. Rick and Kath and I went to see Simon and Garfunkel do an open air concert in Brisbane. One of their songs is called 'The Rock' and the lyrics in part go:

'I am a rock,
I am an island.
And a rock feels no pain,
And an island never cries'.

They were lyrics I aspired to.

I needed to become more of a rock.

In July I was entitled to free travel on the Queensland railways. I had worked for them for six months. I decided to go as far as I could in the two weeks holiday I had booked. I was going to travel on the long slow train up to Cairns, in Northern Queensland. The tracks follow the East coast of Australia, alongside the 'Great Barrier Reef '.

It was a two-day trip of over one thousand miles and passed through small coastal towns with names like Rockhampton, Mackay and Townsville.

On the train journey I got off near a place called Airlie beach between Mackay and Townsville and found a big sailing boat that was going to a small offshore island. There were a few travellers also on board and it was a day in the sun and the wind and it was beautiful beyond words. Big blue sky, golden sands, remote location, freedom.

I got back on another slow train going north the next day and carried on my trip to Cairns.

When I reached Cairns, I booked up in the youth hostel there and met other like-minded travellers. I was in my element.

I went out on another boat to a small sandy island with not even a tree on it. Then I sunbathed on the beach, went in a small glass bottomed boat that was nearby and saw many beautiful coloured fish swimming past and equally exotic coral colours and shapes. I even saw a turtle.

After a couple of days I caught a train further north and then caught a small steam train up onto the Atherton tableland. The tracks wound their way up through the tropical rainforest and stopped at the top, where there was a hippy craft market. I bought a pewter/silver type thick necklace and a strange looking earring to put in my ear. I was having the time of my life.

From there I travelled further North to a very remote area near Cape Tribulation where I stayed for a couple of nights. The beach was idyllic. Palm trees and all that sort of stuff.

When I eventually reached the end of my holiday, I was refreshed and inspired to travel the world some more. It was now August and I had about three weeks left before my visa expired, so I was getting ready to leave Australia and see what lay ahead. I had booked my air ticket to fly back to England, via Sydney, Japan and Alaska. So plenty lay ahead!

Julie and Gary had split up earlier in the year which was sad, but not a surprise in the end. I went out with Gary a few times at the weekends. Once we went fishing in a little two-seater motor boat up an estuary and into the countryside. We ended up running out of petrol and drifting with the current. I had learned how to row with oars when I had worked on the boats at Dartmouth the year before, so I started rowing to the river bank where we could see a house. We managed to get a little petrol and made it back to the boat hire yard near the estuary just as he was shutting the place up... and just as we arrived, the petrol ran out!

Gary told me that he was going back to England in October when his visa ran out. Julie on the other hand, was not going to leave Australia, but instead, go and hide! She didn't want to go back to England to live.

It was while I was with Gary one day at someone's house, that I heard some bad news from my parents back in England. Our dog Cindy had died. She was sixteen years old. We had had Cindy since I was aged seven. So out of my two childhood confidantes, I now only had one. My teddy! If he was ever to be burnt up in a fire, I would have no one left to confide in.

I did a couple more weeks at the railway station, then it was time for me to leave. I sold my Yamaha to Rick, had a going away party and on August 20th got a lift to Brisbane airport. There were a few people who came and said goodbye to me at the airport, even two guys from my first job at Leach Motors. Julie and Gary were there, but not as a couple any more. As I said goodbye to Gary, neither of us knew then, that he would get back to England before me!

The plane flew south to Sydney and I was on the good side for all the views. We banked over to the left and there was the Sydney opera house and the harbour bridge below me.

I was due to meet two travellers I had met in Cairns the previous month. The three of us had realised that we were all independently going to be in Sydney on the 20th of August. So we decided to try and meet up outside the opera house at midday.

It was going to be fun to see if we all made it there and met. This was in the days before mobile phones. Which allowed a bit more creative and unexpected adventure to rumble about in life.

They were both there. The girl was from New Zealand I think and the guy was from Germany and he was called Harry. We spent a few hours together and went up the one-thousand-foot high, Centre Point Tower in the City. We got to see the whole of Sydney from the highest vantage point.

A caricature sketch of me, done by a street artist in Sydney

As it happened, a year or so later I was to again meet up with Harry. But next time the temperature would be different. The next time we would meet it would be 'below minus 20 degrees centigrade'.

We said goodbye to each other at the end of the day and went our separate ways.

My next stop was Tokyo, Japan. I got a bus to Sydney airport and flew to Japan.

When I arrived at the airport near Tokyo, I got on a train into the City. I was tired but I needed to go and explore. Another culture shock. Everyone was shorter than me, so that was new. I walked the back streets with my baggy army trousers, oriental cotton jacket and eyeliner on. I had got into the habit of wearing black eyeliner. It made me more mysterious and that is what I liked to be for some reason.

There were big crowds of people hanging around buildings and I was curious to know what they were doing, so I pushed my way through into one of the buildings. It then became apparent that they were betting houses.

Me in the Buddhist temple complex

I then wandered off the beaten track and found myself in a remote cemetery with all sorts of strange paraphernalia hanging from the tombs. From there I found myself in a huge Buddhist temple complex that was crowded with people. There were various large temples and idols and archways all around. I never really got to the end of it all.

I then realised I needed to get back to the town where the airport was. It was starting to get dark and I could easily have fallen asleep on the train, but I made myself stay awake, because if I missed the station, who knows where I would end up? I definitely didn't want to miss the plane. There was too much at stake, so I didn't go to sleep then! But boy, would I sleep on the plane.

My next destination was Anchorage, Alaska. Now that was going to be interesting! But before that... sleep... zzzzzz.

It was one of those strange times when because of the time difference you arrive somewhere before the time you actually left.

When I got off at Anchorage airport, they gave me a three month visa. So I thought to myself, 'Why not hang about for a few months. I might as well check the place out?'

I got booked into a youth hostel in town and got to know some people and, after a week, six of us rented out a room in the town and just slept on the floor. There was just enough room, and it was way cheaper than staying at the hostel.

Soon after that I was hitching somewhere and a guy picked me up and offered me some work in a factory out in the woods, making wooden window frames. I had a big stapler gun and had to assemble window and door frames. On the way to work I used to buy a loaf of bread (twenty-four slices), a tub of Philadelphia cheese spread and a tin of kidney beans. And during that day I would slowly eat the whole lot. At break times I would just make a sandwich with the cheese and beans and eat it, then another and another. I hardly stopped to talk. I just ate.

Then I would go back to the sleeping den and crash. But near the end of the week I used to go to 'The Metropolitan' nightclub on the edge of Anchorage. It was a place where many black people used to go. I loved going there and dancing. I also frequented a place called 'Chilkoot Charlie's', which was a crazy place. All made from natural tree trunks. It was a popular place to go and people used to get stoned, drink Tequila and listen to music, sometimes bands, sometimes DJs.

Alaska was different from anywhere else I had been before. Beautiful mountains and, in the far distance, I could even see the snow covered peak of Mount McKinley, which is over 20,000ft. high and is the highest mountain in North America. Autumn colours that were stunning, hairy guys driving around in old Ford Chevy trucks, the north American native population mixed in with everyone else, liquor stores, breakfast diners, gun shows, rodeo's, Harley's, chew tobacco, glaciers, big semi-trucks and many more totally unique flavours of life to savour.

I met a New Zealand guy called Greg, who like me was travelling around and we hung out a lot. We used to go off into the mountains in his old red Chevy. He had got it really cheap and it did the job. We used to buy weed and smoke almost every time we met up. Those Autumn colours looked real good to us in the bright sunlight. We used to go to the 'Metropolitan' and dance the night away, even if we were the only two dancing. They played some good tunes in that club. I remember the owner Charles coming over to me and saying, 'It's like you are worshipping when you dance, worshipping some higher being'. I didn't know about that, but he bought me a drink and I was encouraged all the same!

Then Greg introduced me to a couple of his friends that were working behind the bar at 'Chilkoot Charlie's'. They were called Jamie from London, and Vicky from Australia. It was good to meet up with a couple more kindred spirits and Jamie being from England, added an extra bit of kindred.

They lived in a wooden house at the edge of the city as tenants of a girl called Betty. Betty was the same age as us and was a local.

Me and a couple of friends in Alaska

I ended up moving into the house as a tenant too. It was cheaper, cosier and more homely than the sleeping den. We went out and partied quite often and it was when I was with these guys that I first snorted lines of cocaine. Jamie had some good quality gear and offered me some. I was a bit concerned about how addictive this drug is, but he put my mind at ease and assured me that it didn't have to be, so I snorted up the lines and we went off as a group to check out 'Chilkoot Charlie's'. When we got there the DJ put on a song that I had never heard before, called 'Safety Dance', by a group called 'Men without Hats'. It was a new band and a track that was taking off in England apparently.

Well did I get into dancing to that. It was made for me. And even without the cocaine in me it would have caught me. But with the cocaine – I was flying. I flaming loved it. What a night this was!

I felt like some amazing dude, like a god, so confident, so indestructible!

The next day I thought to myself, 'I've got to be very careful. That cocaine is very powerful stuff. I can't afford – in more ways than one, to start liking and depending on it, to boost my life.'

I only ever took it once more in my life. At Glastonbury festival the following year. And the quality was not anywhere near the same as in Alaska. I can see why a lot of performers and jet setters get addicted. It gives a 'convincing', but false sense of security. And makes one come over as being very charismatic.

But it is not only a rich man's drug. Many depend on it, who haven't got the money readily available.

I was going to stay out of its way. I wanted something more dependable than a quick fix!

As October came around the snow started falling. The Autumn colours started fading and the temperature started to drop!

Guys at work were given the opportunity to work one weekend, to fit out a new DIY store. It would be a one-off twelve-hour shift, with triple pay. I went and joined the shift from midday on Saturday, to midnight. We were given free coffee and doughnuts through the shift.

When midnight came around, I was tired, but decided to join the next shift team. It was an opportunity not to be missed. The first crew all went home. And I went on through the early hours alongside the fresh team. After about five hours I started to feel very tired and was struggling. A guy called Dan gave me some 'blue devils' (speed pills). They got me running around like Tigger!

But after about three hours they wore off. And the final few hours till midday on Sunday were a real struggle. I was like a zombie.

I got a lift back into the City and slept for eighteen hours straight without waking up. I finally woke up around 8 am. on the Monday, giving me just enough time to get into work that morning. Boy was that a refreshing sleep!

It was the longest sleep I have ever had in my whole life. Monday was a good day.

When November arrived it became obvious that I should get out of Anchorage before I got totally snowed in. The job came to an end and it was getting colder and people were going out less. I booked my ticket for mid-November. I started saying my goodbyes to the people I had got to know. Jack and Dan at the factory had been good friends and there were various other friends and acquaintances.

A week before I left, on a particularly grey and dreary day I caught a train off into the wild and cold tundra. The tracks followed the big river upstream, past a glacier and past the snow-covered mountains and trees. I was going to a place called Whittier, which was inaccessible by road. The only access was by train, through a long tunnel, or by sea, because it was deep inside a hidden inlet in amongst the mountains. It was a hidden military base in World War Two.

It was a very bleak and depressing place, not helped by the sleet and the overcast conditions at that time of year.

If you missed the train back, you had to wait a week for the next one to get you out of there. So I was very diligent with my timekeeping that day!

There was one big concrete high rise with about seven storeys. It was where the two hundred or so population lived. And that was about all that was there really, apart from the railway station and a few other nondescript buildings. The whole location was surrounded with sheer mountain cliffs. It was inaccessible. And it took about fifteen minutes to look around the place. I reckon there was a lot of boredom in that community. I was told there was a lot of depression there. I bet there was!

When I got back on that train and emerged out of the tunnel the other side, there was a tangible sense of relief coursing through my veins. I was free again. I'm not joking!

It started to get dark before I arrived back in Anchorage and when the train reached its destination, I was pleased to be back around normality.

On the 13th November I got on the plane that would take me back to England. As it flew over the vast inhospitable cold landscape below, I was relieved to be just observing it all through the tiny plane window next to me. I was warm and cosy high up there, out of its reach.

I had been away from England for fifteen months and it was good to be back. What changes would I notice as I started to move amongst my old friends and familiar haunts?

The autumn leaves were still around, mostly on the floor, but still around and still holding onto their rich yellow and brown blaze of colour. I walked around the leaves taking photos with my SLR camera. Photography had captured my interest in Australia when someone I met introduced me to the advantages of an SLR camera. All I had known before was my old Kodak Instamatic camera that I was given as a kid. The photos I used to take, never came up to what I had seen through the viewfinder. The actual photo image was always too small when I received the photos back from processing.

This person I met explained that with an SLR camera, I actually look through the lens itself as I take a photo, so the image I get back as a photo is exactly the same as the image I saw when I took the photo. This was revolutionary for me. I had seen other people's photos and they always looked so much better than mine.

I had bought a second-hand Ricoh SLR camera. And when I got back to England I quickly bought a zoom lens and a wide-angle lens.

So I was continually panning the landscape for beautiful and interesting images to capture. I had a new and fairly addictive hobby!

I went back and lived with my parents in St Marychurch. They hadn't moved. And they were still doing the same jobs. Robert was nearly sixteen and was in his last year at secondary school.

It was good to start catching up with my old mates. Some relationships had ended and other relationships had started up, some that would ultimately result in marriage. One such wedding was to take place a few days after I got back to England.

Now returned, a bunch of us got together on Paignton seafront under the old Festival Theatre café. It was so good to swap stories about what had happened since I had been away. The 'Meps' had grown in members. Ken, Dan, Abo and Jonny, had joined. The 'Y society' club that they had been in before, had come to an end. It was a natural step for them to join the 'Meps', because we all used to hang out with each other anyway. Then Adrian and Jim and a few others I knew from before, had also joined the club.

There were 'Mephistopheles' patches on a lot of coat sleeves now. Some of the club had even had it tattooed on their arms.

The bikes were different too. The British bikes were mainly gone, the big four-cylinder Jap bikes taking their place. And the style had changed. There were now, mean-looking low rider chops, with big 1000cc engines.

The whole scene had taken on a new look. And it looked good.

People were interested in what I had been doing in Australia and Alaska. It was good to be around familiar faces and friends.

The following weekend Ken, from the club, and Dawn got married. It was a good rendezvous for a lot of us. All dressed up in suits, with plenty of bikes to create a backdrop for some of the wedding photos.

I realised at this time that I was not going to buy a big bike and slot back into the same scene. I had been away and I had changed.

Me having some fun with my old Mephistopheles mates:
(left to right) Magg, Jerry, Gord, Jon, Ross, Scott, Me, Dena

I still wanted to hang out with the guys, but not in the full-blown biker way that I had before. I had saved enough money while I had been away to get a really nice bike, but my interest in bikes was not so important now.

The money I had saved was going to support my life of wandering around the world. I was still on a mission. And I had only partially entered into it.

There was so much further to go, and that wasn't just geographically!

Christmas time arrived. And soon after, the New Year's Eve party. It was at Lawson's flat. It was a cool place to meet up. With a touch of Bohemia around the place. I now liked to dress up in a sort of mysterious style of my own now, mixed with a 'new romantic' style.

I went dressed up in my new black baggy Bowie trousers, black suede pointed winklepickers and white cotton Japanese shirt. I had cut lines into the sides of my hair with an electric shaver, which I had first done out in Alaska. I had on my hippy silver/pewter style necklace and a tarnished silver capsule earing. My important black eyeliner finished the look.

I can't say I particularly fitted in with the biker image that was prominent in the place that night but my mates just took it in their stride. 'It's Mark, being weird!'

The party was good and there were quite a few new people on the scene.

This New Year's Eve party was a lot less lonely than the last one (in Brisbane). It was good to be around old friends.

1984

Early on in the New Year I started to build a darkroom in my bedroom. I built a wooden framed structure within the room. Then I bought some heavy duty black plastic sheet and stapled it to the sides and top of the frame. It was 5ft long, 4ft wide, 6ft high. This was to be my photographic darkroom! I bought all the equipment I needed to roll my own film into cartridges, develop film and print photos onto various sizes of photographic paper.

Also early on in the New Year I bought a small red Honda XL250 trail bike with an XR front end. It was to be my transport and not a status image this time.

My image now seemed to be wrapped up in how I dressed and looked. I was always on the lookout for strange clothes and hats. I was buzzing about on my ego. I was often full of myself. Sometimes right out there, being a party animal but at other times desperately lonely.

I bought a dull red crochet woollen type of hat. It was a strange sort of thing that had lots of pieces of wool that looked like hair and that could be arranged to look very crazy. It was full on! I used to wear it to certain parties. With my eyes enhanced with black eyeliner, I was quite a spectacle and didn't blend in with the crowd at all. I was still smoking weed fairly often, so it all mixed into the weirdness. There were even days when I would walk down through town like this. On one occasion I stuck a small digital clock to my nose and dressed up in some strange gear, including the red hat/wig. I even stuck on some false plastic eyelashes too I seem to remember.

As I went down through the town like a crazy man, my heart was beating, but there was something about being under a mask, that empowered me. It also brought me a lot of attention. There was definitely something I liked about that too. I wanted to be noticed (obviously!), I wanted to be Significant, I didn't want to be ignored. And I was out there looking for the magic solution.

But, I never found it, everything was only ever a quick fix. Then I was alone again.

A lot of my time was spent going around on my bike taking black and white photos to develop and print in my homemade darkroom.

I had come upon this idea in my head that my photos were going to become popular and much sought after. And that this fame was going to finance my travels around the world. My name as a photographer was going to be 'Eidaw Kram'. I was going to have a studio and café in London and people would be waiting for the new 'Eidaw Kram Collection': photos from Peru, or Africa, or wherever I had just been.

The collection was going to comprise of five specially framed photos from that country. Only fifty sets would be available, at a high cost. And each set came with a smaller framed 'Eidaw Kram' special motif plaque that signified the set was complete.

So I had a plan. Like those early days as child, I once again had a dream. Back then it was about football, now it was about being a famous photographer. The reality might turn out to be different, but we have to dream, yeah? Dreams spur us on to greater things.

Problem is illusions of grandeur can often start feeding our egos. So, I was 'buzzing about on my ego'. Much too much.

(If you hadn't noticed 'Eidaw Kram' was my name backwards.)

My plans took me to London for a few days, to take some more photos. I met up with Jamie (who I had lived with in Alaska). We went around together to beaten up areas of London where I snapped away. I had borrowed another wide-angle lens from a friend and by fixing it to my wide-angle lens managed to create a fisheye lens that made the photos into a round image and distorted the objects I took photos of.

I got right into this new perspective. Especially after Jamie and me had smoked a joint.

I also took different photos of the River Thames from different vantage points. One photo of Tower Bridge from the old docklands (years before the area was all rebuilt), appeared in my darkroom developing tray with a real quality to it.

But the reality was, I wasn't that good at photography. I had had no training at College so I was an amateur really. I was just excited about what the SLR camera could do. And I had my own darkroom.

The enthusiasm, which is a big part of my character, carried me off into a realm that I didn't 'belong' to. But that road of discovery, still had to be walked down for a while, before it would end at a brick wall entitled, 'You're not going to be a world-famous photographer'.

Another feature of this year was buying a Reliant Regal three-wheeler van. Some people may not remember these vehicles, but they were particularly useful for people that hadn't passed their driving test, but had passed their full motorbike test.

And that person, was me!

What a buzz it was to at last drive around the place, protected from the elements. It was a shabby old thing, the whole body being made of fibreglass, but I loved it. It was a bit unstable going round sharp corners fast, as I was to find out soon enough, but basically it kept me dry, warm and in good humour!

Smoking pot and grass was becoming a bit of a regular habit and I regularly get paranoid about situations and people. But another problem with taking drugs, was that I was not getting off to do what I had planned to do with my life. Leave England and wander around the world on my own.

The trouble with the drugs was they were keeping me on the roundabout. I was going round and round the same pattern of life each day, but never taking an exit. I was caught up in believing that they were helping me suss out what life was all about, in fact exactly the opposite was true.

I needed to get off the roundabout and take an exit.

But for now – I wasn't strong enough.

There were plenty of parties going on in this season it seemed and sometimes they were quite eventful. In the story that follows, the eventfulness was more in getting to, and leaving the party.

This particular party was down at the 'Drum Inn', in Cockington, which is a lovely little tourist suburb country hamlet at the edge of Torquay. I had my three-wheeler van and I was all dressed up in my weird attire. On the way to the party I picked up two good friends from the 'Meps', Jerry and Adrian. We went up to Gallows gate before going on to the party. This was a secluded viewpoint overlooking the Bay and not too far from the 'Drum Inn'. We went there first, so that we could smoke some gear and get in the party mood. Well it turned into quite an adventure soon after the smoke. I decided to go in reverse with the Reliant van (Jerry was in the front and Adrian cramped in the back). But there was more to the operation than just reverse! I decided to lock the steering wheel to the left and go round and round in circles, and for good measure, press the horn continually at the same time.

Who said men can't multitask! This was obviously no normal man!

Well we got a bit dizzy and then it was time to do something different. I set off down a little country road, that I was sure ended down in the valley at Cockington. On the way down the road I was being a drug-fuelled clown as usual.

A right-hand bend was upon us and as I turned to go round it (do remember my van has only one front wheel – an important fact at this point), we went up onto two wheels, the rear right now off the floor by quite a way. Next thing we were scraping along the tarmac on the left side of the fibreglass body (all three wheels are now NOT in relationship with the road).

The next stage of the journey was upside-down and scraping along the tarmac with the roof of the van (all three wheels are well up in the air now!)

And then we came into contact with the hedge and a lot of the green material that dwells therein.

Then we stop. The engine is still running, even upside-down. At this point I have lost my drug-induced wellbeing. In its place is now panic. I am hanging upside-down by my seatbelt, unable to get out. Oil and petrol are dripping everywhere and I am going to be burnt alive in this fibreglass capsule. Amazing how quick one can go from having fun… to… not having fun.

Meanwhile Jerry and Adrian have got out somehow. And somehow I worked myself free of the seatbelt, then managed to force the door open, switch off the engine and get out. I stood up and looked at the chassis of the car and then looked at Jerry and Adrian. They were silent – watching to see how I would respond to this dire situation.

The drug-induced clown, now with 'added' adrenalin, responded, 'Let's keep this party going!'

We laughed out loud and proceeded to turn the van the proper way up (wheels back down). The front windscreen was half-out due to the roof being pulled back, the door pillars were cracked, there were sticky weeds and other green vegetation all over the place, mixed in with hot black engine oil. The engines on Reliant three-wheelers are predominantly inside the driving cab of the car. And on top of the interior engine cover is an ashtray, so the oil from the engine when it was upside-down, had come out, gone through the ashtray and dripped onto the interior ceiling of the car. So it was a right mess inside, as well as out.

I had a few pints of spare oil in the back, so I poured it all in. Then I started the engine and it ran, but there was a click click click coming from the engine compartment. Then we set off again down the road. Trouble was – the road didn't end up in Cockington. It ended up at the front of a big farmhouse. It was a dead end road. We needed to turn around and head back up the road we had come from, but first I needed to find out what that clicking noise was. It sounded pretty serious!

As I got out of the vehicle, to open the small hatch at the front of the van, the farmer who owned the farm arrived in his car and he wasn't happy. I think he had seen us at the top of the hill going round in circles backwards, with the horn going. And now he was looking at us three, adorned with vegetation and black oil. Jerry and Adrian started keeping him occupied, while I frantically looked inside the engine compartment to see if I could see where the clicking noise was coming from. Then I saw it! It was the oil dipstick. When we were upside-down, it must have come out of its hole and was now caught up with rotating metal fan blades at the front of the engine. I was really happy it was easy to fix and, as I was attempting to put the dipstick back into its hole, the farmer continued ranting at Jerry and Adrian. He could see the van was smashed up and the windscreen was out and weeds and oil were all over it. And I thought, 'He is going to call the police soon if we don't get out of here quick.' Then I suddenly located the hole for the dipstick and put it back in. The farmer kept saying, 'What on earth is going on here?'

Now with the dipstick back in and the clicking noise gone, I was able to reply with, 'Everything's fine, it was just the dipstick caught up in the fan.' And with that, we quickly got back in the van and got out of there as quick as we could.

We had a party to attend!

Man, when we turned up at that party, we were flying. We had been to the moon and back! Boy did we have a story to tell!!?

I can't remember much more about the actual party, but the night was not over when the party finished.

We were off to somewhere else and some friends needed a lift!

And I had my van. It was in a mess but it was still going.

There were seven of us in that van as we left the 'Drum Inn' that night. If you know Reliant Regal's, you know that is a lot of people!

That is another problem with drugs. Wrong decisions are made. and taking seven people in a Reliant Regal van that has been upside-down, earlier in the evening… is a wrong decision.

As I started to climb the very steep narrow country road out of Cockington the van slowed down… slowed down… slowed down… then a loud noise came from it, and it was dead. And I mean dead, the engine never lived again.

I think someone must have towed me with a rope the following day to my home in St Marychurch. It certainly wasn't going anywhere on its own power.

I ended up going with my brother Robert to a house in Hele (another area of Torquay) where I had seen a dumped Reliant car in the rear garden. We walked there with my Dad's wheelbarrow. In the wheelbarrow were my tools. The guy at the house said we could have the engine out of the dumped car for a small sum of money. Robert and I tipped the car on its side, took the engine out and walked back to our house with it in the wheelbarrow.

We lifted the front end of my car up, removed the old engine and fitted the other one. It was a bit of a job and needed the help of Dad and Robert underneath. I stood on top of the bonnet with a rope, lifting it into position.

It ended up being a good engine and did me proud for the rest of the time I owned the vehicle.

I took the cylinder head off the old engine, to just see what the problem was. The top of one of the pistons had totally come off and had made a big mess inside the bore. It was definitely dead!

In June I went to Glastonbury music festival. A few people were going from Torquay. I ended up going with Adrian in a white transit van that was owned by someone we knew called John. John was a market trader and had a stall booked at the festival. When we reached the queue at the gate, Adrian and I got in the back underneath all of John's stuff and hid. We didn't want to pay to get in.

The festival was well-attended as always and I secretly felt quite lonely and self-conscious. The drugs were not helping the situation. The paranoia was setting in.

At the start I had taken some cocaine. But it wasn't anywhere near the same quality as the stuff in Alaska. Then I smoked pot with various people I knew, but that didn't help my sense of wellbeing.

I ended up wearing my over-the-top, red, crochet woollen hat and I put on my mirror shades to keep my eyes hidden. And that combination did the trick. People didn't dare look at this strange looking man with a crazy hat, mirror shades, a small beard and an assortment of unusual clothing.

I had found a way to move amongst this huge crowd, with a secure disposition, using this mystery disguise.

There were a couple of incidents that threw me though. One was a dog running up behind me and biting both my knees from behind. Why me? It was enough to give me a complex for a few hours, plus it hurt for a while too.

The other thing was a 'hash cookie'. Trouble with eating hash and not smoking it is there is no way you can properly regulate the amount that you are letting in your body. When you smoke it, you can get a gradual sense of where you're at with the trip. But when you eat it, it is not a gradual hit. It is just a hit!

I ended up going on a horrible paranoia trip. The details of which – I won't bore telling you about. But it was another very lonely experience.

While I was at the festival I bumped into Greg from Clevedon, who was in the 'Meps'. He was in a tent enjoying some dope. I joined him and his friends. After leaving that tent I didn't see him again for exactly thirty years. In June 2014, I set off on a mission to find him again, without the use of any social media.

It's a lot more fun doing it without social media. It forces you to talk to a lot of strangers, I can tell you!

The 'Smiths' were a big attraction for that year's festival.

Apart from that, I remember very little.

After Glastonbury, I decided to write out a promise to myself. I dated it and signed it. No one knew about it but me. It was a secret promise to help start getting my life together a bit more.

I promised myself that I would take no more drugs after my birthday on July 9th. I would be twenty-four years old.

If I was going to get off the roundabout and take an exit road, I needed to stop taking drugs.

I didn't have a serious habit or anything like that, but I would smoke on my own every few days, and if I was at other people's houses and they were smoking joints, which they often were, I would join in.

One of the things with getting high on drugs I found, was that I would get lost in the little things. I would be fascinated with the minuscule details around me and get absorbed with them. But what I would lose out on, was the overall perspective of life. I would focus on what was growing in the middle of the roundabout, as it were! Going round that roundabout became a pattern.

Somehow I knew the answer wasn't inside the roundabout.

I needed to stop taking drugs. And I couldn't play about, procrastinating about the way forward for my life.

On my birthday I went with friends to the 'Cavern' bar, a good night club by the harbour. It was underground under another pub and the ambience was very 'underground' too.

It was popular with punks, bikers, skinheads, new romantics, teddy boys and anyone else who was alternative at heart.

And there were hardly any fights. They did occur, but were surprisingly rare. There was a mutual respect for each other. The music was varied and it was a great place to go. And I fitted in fine!

It was my last official day for taking drugs. I think I snorted a couple of lines of speed that night.

That night took an unexpected turn for me. And it was totally unexpected. One of the people I knew there that night was a girl called Elaine. I had met her once earlier in the year. Back then she was going out with a guy who was around the biker scene and was older than me. We started chatting and she told me that their relationship was over now. Somehow we both knew that we liked each other quite a lot. The next thing, we were kissing away, as the music and the atmosphere around us went on its own way. We were lost in each other and at the same time, found in each other! It was good.

The next day Elaine appeared at my house and it appeared she wanted to be with me. I was slightly hesitant deep inside, because I was starting to get the feel that I would soon be getting my plan together. The 'Eidaw Kram' collection, and then wander the world, on my own! Especially now that I was stopping the drugs.

But at the end of the day, this was a turn of events that was too good to miss out on. Elaine was an attractive and adventurous girl. She seemed to be a kindred spirit.

So I went with it. And it was good to be together. It was good to have company.

In a year from now, I was going to be in a totally different setting, with some other company I would never have expected!

But it's good we don't know the future. If we did, life would get very boring, with no surprises and no adventures. Unknown horizons lure us. They woo us to adventure. They woo us to bigger discoveries, about what is behind them and also about who we are inside ourselves.

They allow us to search.

And this new relationship with Elaine was also going to allow me to search. I was definitely on a journey.

A few weeks after my birthday, I did smoke another joint. (Breaking the promise I had made to myself.)

It was at that point I woke up to the fact that the drugs were controlling me. If I couldn't even make a pledge to myself, it was a serious situation.

And the realisation of that, actually DID wake me up.

I stopped taking drugs.

Around this time I was on a government enterprise working scheme. For three days a week a crew of us would go out to nearby towns and villages and do things like painting and decorating. Before my birthday, there were days when we would get stoned and haphazardly drift through the work.

With my new resolve to stop taking drugs, those days were over.

Now I was on a mission. To get an exit road off the roundabout and explore the world, outside of Torquay, beyond Devon and away from England.

I liked England, but there was more. There was more freedom to be found and I was going to search for it. Because if I was honest, I knew I wasn't free.

Elaine and I used to go off together in the three-wheeler van. This was enjoyable for a time but I needed more in my life than just exploring Devon and having fun taking black and white photos. Around August time, my friend Greg (New Zealander) who I had hung out with in Alaska the previous year, came to visit me in Torquay.

He stayed for a few days and Elaine and I showed him the sights. One day the three of us went together up into the middle of Dartmoor, in the Reliant. Greg was also into photography and it was a great day. I had never got to say goodbye to him in Alaska because he had been arrested (for working illegally) and was deported the same day. That had been a big shock and he never got the opportunity to say goodbye to anybody. Now we had time to swap stories and catch up.

A lot of my free time was spent in my darkroom. Sometimes I would spend over twelve hours in there and only come out to go to the toilet. It was fascinating to alter the compositions and shades with the enlarger and then see how the photos would materialise in front of my eyes in the processing liquid. I had now compiled five prints for the 'Eidaw Kram River Thames Collection', and five prints for the 'Devon Castles Collection'.

I had also got hundreds of snazzy round stickers made. They were four inches in diameter and had a large photo of my eye in the middle that followed you about (if you know what I mean). Around the outside of the sticker were the words, 'Eidaw Kram Collection'. I went around all over the place putting these stickers up, when no one was looking! A bit like when people put up illegal posters, to advertise their gig or event.

My reasoning was that as people saw my stickers, they would become intrigued and curious to find out what it was all about. And gossip would start up, creating a platform for me to present the collections to the world at the appropriate time. The appetite would precede me! That was the idea anyway!

I invented my own design of a wooden frame that stood off the wall by about an inch. I bought 100 pieces of special thick coloured card cut as a background for the 10 by 8 inch photos.

Then I bought all the non-reflective glass that fitted my handmade frames. Plus chrome clips to clip the glass to the frames.

I had also created an 'Eidaw Kram' ink stamp that I stamped each coloured card with. Then there was the smaller glass framed souvenir plaque, that went with each collection of five prints.

I got right into it. I even made a special handmade wooden box lined with foam to transport them about in.

It sort of took over from my joy of taking photos and creating effects in the darkroom.

I think the business ego thing overtook the art and creativity. It was sad really. But it was part of the necessary journey I needed to take in my life at that time.

In the Autumn I started looking for a temporary flat of my own. Mum and Dad were hoping to leave their rented house in St Marychurch and get their own place. They had been given an opportunity to get a mortgage again. And it seemed an appropriate time for me to get my own space.

I got a flat up on a hill behind Wellswood, in Torquay. It was functional and included a TV, that could end up being too easy to watch. Yes it's got an 'off' switch, but a box of chocolates has also got a lid! Not always a big enough deterrent.

Also around the Autumn time Elaine and I had gone to Suffolk to stay with a couple that she knew. They were about our age and the guy was a professional photographer. He was good and had all the gear. We all used to go for walks in the fields around their house and for the first time in my life I got to see English long-eared hares running about.

One night I got really drunk at the local pub. We all got back to the house. But I had a bad night. I think my relationship with Elaine was getting stretched and cracks were starting to come up. She seemed to want to know where I actually was, in the relationship. And that was something I didn't want to explore too deeply.

By the end of November this question was hanging in the air quite heavily. And basically, I couldn't assure Elaine that I was wholeheartedly in the relationship, so I decided to end it.

More was needed of me and I couldn't give it. There was a part of me that I couldn't seem to give away. Not just to Elaine, but to anyone! It had been a recurring problem in past relationships too.

I was quite self-contained deep down inside of me. I didn't want to let go of it to any other person. And even possibly, couldn't.

It is only now looking back that I can rationalise this dilemma. Back then, I didn't have a clue!

All I did know, was that I needed to become more of a *rock*. I knew another person could not become a *rock* for me. That was not the answer.

By December, Dad's job at the Palace Hotel had come to an end and he was now working as a gardener at the Imperial Hotel, which was beautifully located overlooking the bay.

Also in this month, Mum and Dad were about to move out of their rented house. They had found an affordable small terraced house in the Chelston area of Torquay, and a shorter ten-year mortgage (because of their age) had been arranged.

They had booked a big rental van that Dad was looking forward to driving on the removal day. The whole move was going to be done and dusted before Christmas.

The day before the move, I was in my new flat and there was a knock at the window. It was Robert. He had cycled from Mum and Dad's house and he looked very serious. I ran to the door, but already, I knew what he was going to say. I knew it was bad and I knew it was Dad.

I said, 'It's Dad isn't it!' And he said, 'Yes.'

Dad was in hospital in Plymouth. He had had a brain haemorrhage.

I rushed into my bedroom to get my shoes. As I entered the room, I nearly broke down in tears and something instinctively came out of my mouth. The words that came out must have come from somewhere deep inside me. They must have been well tucked away, because I had no idea they were even there.

'God, please don't let Dad die.'

I rushed back out to Robert, put his bicycle in the back of the van, and drove over to the house in St Marychurch.

Poor Mum. It was all happening. It was quite a serious situation. Dad was alive, but we would have to wait, to see how he was.

Mum asked me if I had a friend who could drive the removal rental van the next day. It was a big van with a tail lift and she was not comfortable about driving it. I had actually passed my test the previous month, but the rental agreement stipulated that anyone who drove the van needed to have had a full licence for a whole year.

So I asked my friend Dave. He was an old biker mate that I had recently been meeting up with.

It was a long day, all pulling together to get the stuff out of the house and transporting it to the other side of town. There was a lot of stuff, as there nearly always is. But doing it with Dave, Robert and Mum was fun. We felt quite a close team, by the time we completed the move. Mum operated well in all the drama of the situation. She really came into her own. I think it brought back her old nursing instincts.

The next day mum went to the Plymouth hospital. Dad was resting and had somehow survived his ordeal. He was happy to hear that the move had been successful.

After a week or so, he was released from hospital and returned to the new house with a white bandage wrapped around his head.

The four of us enjoyed Christmas together. Dad was on the mend. After a few weeks he was back to normal.

While Dave was helping out with the house move, he told me that the job he was doing was really good fun. He was working for a government enterprise company called 'Small Woodlands', in Dartington, near Totnes. Another old biker mate I knew called Maestro, was also working for them, and the job entailed thinning out overgrown woodlands in the countryside. The crew were apparently good people and the company paid for some staff to train for, and obtain, the certificate that was needed to use a chainsaw. I liked the sound of this job. It was three days a week, the same as the one I was doing, but it sounded a lot more fulfilling, and fun too. I told him I would like a job there.

Dave asked them if they had any jobs for me and a vacancy came up in mid-January.

I left my existing job just before Christmas. So I was free for a couple of weeks.

The day after Boxing day, I packed my sleeping bag, some blankets and some clothes into the van and set off on an adventure.

I was going to drive to Southern Germany and find Harry, the German guy I had met up with outside Sydney opera house, in August '82.

It was going to be a long cold trek, but it was the thing to do.

I had his address in Ulm and I corresponded by letter to confirm it was OK, and that he would be there.

I drove to Dover and crossed over the English Channel to France. As I was driving off the ferry into Calais I was thinking to myself, 'this could be a long, slow, monotonous drive.'

But all that changed in my thinking when the French people who caught sight of me were taken aback with some sort of glee. Many had not seen such a strange vehicle as my old Reliant. The sight of my three-wheeler van caused them to smile, wave, and quickly get the attention of their friends before I was out of sight.

If they were close enough to actually see me, with my beard, hat and eye liner, well that was the icing on the cake for them. So it ended up being fun, watching for people's reactions and waving at them.

As it got dark, I started to get tired and there was still a long way to go to reach Ulm, so I stopped for the night.

I found a place to park up the Reliant away from houses, then I folded the passenger seat forward and lay down in the back of the van. The van is short and my feet were basically up by the front windscreen, but I was dry and hopefully safe.

In December of 1984 it was very cold in Germany. I had been wearing lots of clothes, and even gloves on the drive south, but in the night the temperature dropped even more. I had brought a few blankets in preparation, and I needed them all that night.

The next morning it was clear and sunny and I spent the rest of that day driving on down to Ulm.

I eventually found Harry's house, which turned out to be on an island by the banks of the River Danube.

He was amazed I had driven all the way down from England, especially in the peculiar vehicle in front of him. He had not even seen such a car. It was quite a celebrity in that neighbourhood while I was around. Germany was another totally new experience for me and soon after I arrived, snow started falling and the country was gripped in a big freeze. It was picturesque to look at and gave me plenty of subject

154

matter for photos. The days were often sunny and brought out the rich colour contrasts, so it was a good thing I had taken colour film to Germany. Now although sunny, the days were extremely cold. I remember well the walks I would go on by myself along the banks of the River Danube and watching huge lumps of ice moving along with the current. Not enough to totally cover the water, but not far off. When I breathed in through my nose, the hairs inside my nostrils immediately turned to ice, and I then had to squeeze my nose with my gloved hands to melt the ice inside. It was minus 21°C.

But those walks were really invigorating and made me feel alive.

Soon after my arrival it was New Year's Eve and the people of Ulm were all prepared. As I was to find out at midnight!

1985

As the bells chimed, the firework display started up and what a display, they really went to town. With the old city as a backdrop, it was a spectacular and beautiful way to usher in the new year.

Those fireworks marked the start of a very important year in my life.

Within twelve hours, Harry and I were off in his car to see some sights in nearby Switzerland. There was snow all around but it only added to the occasion. We drove on the shores of Lake Constance and carried on during the day until we arrived at 'Rhine Falls' in Switzerland. The mighty river Rhine was in full flow as it carried huge blocks of ice down it's cascading falls.

We then drove to the city of Freiburg in the South West corner of Germany where we spent the night with some friends of Harry who lived in an impressive flat that overlooked some equally impressive architectural buildings below.

I stayed in Germany a few more days back at Harry's flat, and one day, Harry and I climbed to the top of one of the high spires of Ulm Cathedral. It was a long and cold climb and I was very pleased to reach the end when we did. It was high, but the views of the snow-covered city were amazing and made the nerve-racking climb well worth it.

Over the next few days I met a few of Harry's friends, but as they socialised, mainly using the German language, I started to feel quite isolated and self-conscious in their company.

When the time came for me to leave, I was quite relieved as I could now be on my own again and not have to feel awkward.

The weather had deteriorated during my stay, and the news headlines were of lorries coming off the Autobahns because of the blizzards and extreme icy conditions. It was one of the worst winters in memory and Harry wondered if I would make it back to England safely, but I was ready to leave and I planned to go slowly and carefully.

The drive through Europe on the way back was especially cold and, to anyone who doesn't know, the interior heating system on a Reliant three-wheeler is non-existent.

So my feet and hands were always very cold.

But hey! I was not on a motorbike and for that very reason, I was grateful for every bit of fibre glass that was around me. I was in luxury!

The roads were indeed snowy and icy during the whole journey, but clear enough for me to pass through.

However, as I reached Calais I hit a bad patch of ice and the van went up onto two wheels, with the third wheel high up in the air. I gasped and held my breath as it didn't roll over, but also didn't return to the ground. The outcome was on a knife edge!

The van fell down with a big bump. Amazingly the correct way up. I had survived, through no skill of my own! Crazy isn't it? I drive all that way and at the finishing line – that happened!

After the ferry trip across the channel it felt good to be back in England, and as I drove west through Kent, it became apparent that the snow had also hit my own country. Against the crisp blue sky and the bright green grass, the scenery was *ripe* for a photo, so I ate it up with my camera!

After a few days back in Torquay, I was looking forward to starting my new job at 'Small Woodlands'. I had been thinking about it as I drove back through Europe. It was going to be fun working with a couple of my old biker mates in the woods.

It would also earn me a bit more money before I left England and continued to wander the world.

The job did indeed come up to my hopes. A team of about twelve men and women used to meet at the Huxhams Cross workshop, near Dartington, in the mornings. We would gather into two Land Rovers, with chainsaws, cans of petrol and oil, maintenance tools, protective clothing, helmets, waterproof gear, steel toe-cap boots, ropes, chains, pulleys, axes, bow saws, sledge hammers, wedge splitters, first aid kits, and finally ourselves.

Then we would drive out to some remote woodland site, split into teams and start thinning and clearing the trees as required by the landowners. Often the sites would be on a slope, so one team would start cutting up the large felled tree trunks; another team would fix a rope around the trunk and pull it up the slope using a pulley system and a Land Rover. It was then unclipped and ready for splitting. Meanwhile another team was building bonfires using the smaller branch debris.

It was invigorating work and we would get hot, even though it was in winter. It was fulfilling work too, we would drive back to Dartington at the end of the day and feel very satisfied with what we had done. We had such fun together too. It was a good job.

I got my chainsaw certificate fairly early on, so was also able to get involved with the chainsaw duties.

One of the crew was called Dave and I used to give him a lift into work and back each day, because he lived in Torquay. We have kept in touch over the years and both have good memories of our time with 'Small Woodlands'.

As the Spring started emerging the time at work became even more pleasant. Snowdrops appeared, then crocuses, and next would come the bluebells.

This job, like I said earlier, was only three days a week and suited me fine, because It gave me time to try and launch the 'Eidaw Kram Collection'. I had managed to get a couple of places to put the collections on permanent display in Torquay and Paignton, but to be honest the whole process became quite soul-destroying. One big department store that I was hoping would be interested, declined. I had a meeting with the manager but after showing him the collection he showed no real interest at all.

The fact of the matter was, the photos were nothing too special, and this truth was firmly hitting home. Although I did sell some of my other photos to various people, I'm embarrassed to say that I actually sold none from my 'Eidaw Kram Collection'.

I eventually woke up to the reality that 'Eidaw Kram' fame, was not going to finance my wandering around the world.

It was time for me to take the exit off the roundabout, because I had been going round it for over a year now.

I needed to get away from the stagnant pond of normality and go and find out if I really was a 'rock'. It was easy being a rock in the safe environment of friends and family, but who was I when I was away from all that? Who was I when I was alone and out of my comfort zone, away from the people I knew?

I needed to go out there into the unknown and test myself. I wanted to be a man of substance.

I knew the answer wasn't in another person, because people aren't dependable enough. I knew it wasn't in having loads of money, because if it was, rich people wouldn't commit suicide. I knew it wasn't in a career, because that can just go at any time, and I knew it wasn't in drugs or partying, that had become apparent.

All these things seemed to me, to be like lumps of wood. They would keep me afloat for a time, but then they would get waterlogged, and start sinking. They would become boring, not buoyant, and not able to keep me afloat through life.

Travelling was the big lump of wood that wouldn't sink, it would always be offering exciting experiences, giving me the freedom I was looking for. That was what was missing in my life.

I informed Ian, my manager at 'Small Woodlands' that I would be leaving at the end of April, and he was interested in buying my Honda XL 250 trail bike, so that was good.

He asked me why I wanted to travel: was it because I wanted to see famous sights and stuff like that? I said, 'No it's for other reasons.'

He then said something that got under my skin and niggled me.

He was not being horrible, he was just saying it out of concern I think.

He said, 'Well, as long as you know why you're travelling. It seems to me that a lot of people I meet who travel, are just lost souls.'

I think I got defensive and reassured him that I wasn't a lost soul. Far from it!

But those words did not disappear. They stayed around and haunted me. Not intensely, but they stuck.

My old friend Magg and I painted my shabby light blue Reliant to make it more saleable. The colour we hand painted it with wasn't one that I particularly chose, but it was one I had lying about. It was gloss paint for use on wood I think. But it did the trick and there was just enough! It was Tank Grey!

I started saying my goodbyes to various friends.

Gordon, one of the original 'Meps' and a good friend, said to me a day or so before I left, 'Mark, we are always here for you.'

It was a touching sentiment and one I probably didn't let touch me too much. I needed to be a 'rock'.

I purchased an open train ticket to travel through Europe. It would ultimately end in Athens. I bought about £3000 worth of travellers cheques, and got my friend Philly to sew a secret pocket into the back of my coat, to hide them in.

Ian, from 'Small Woodlands' ended up buying my Honda. On the final evening in Torquay, I sold my Reliant to a Spanish guy in Paignton who had never driven before! He was going to learn, he said.

May 5th was the day of roundabout exit. And I was up for it.

My loose plan was to get to Athens and from there, maybe go to Israel and work on a Kibbutz for a short while. Then when I was confident and ready, leave and start wandering the world.

The answer was to be found... out there somewhere.

My Mum's last words to me as I left the doorstep of the house were, 'I hope you find what you're looking for Mark.'

I then got on the back of Jerry's low rider and he took me and my bag to Torquay coach Station. The next time I saw him, I had a story to tell!

The coach took me to London and I stayed the night with a relative called Brian.

The next day I got on a train to Dover and crossed over to France on the ferry. I was on my way at last. Now I was free. I had no return ticket and no need to return. It was an open-ended adventure and I would see how and where it led.

This was the life I had sampled a taste of, three years before, when I was in France on holiday with my 'Meps' friends. This was how I wanted to live every day, not just on holiday.

It had taken me three years of saving money, and getting waylaid sometimes, but now the time had arrived, the world was my oyster!

I got on a train to Paris and when I arrived I started just walking about. I went to the river Seine, Notre Dame Cathedral, the Louvre, saw the Mona Lisa, went up the Eiffel Tower, and basically soaked up the whole new experience I was now living in.

I didn't know where I would sleep that night and, as the evening went on, no available accommodation was presenting itself to me.

I ended up hiding under small bushes on some land near a tower block complex. I didn't feel that safe, but I was very tired and it was safer than walking the streets. When I was sure no one had seen me and it was dark, I fell asleep.

In the morning when I awoke, my sleeping bag was in amongst dog dirt! Not the perfect first night on the road, but, I was out of my comfort zone! And that is what I wanted, wasn't it?

I left Paris the next day on a night train going south to Genoa on the Mediterranean coast. I found an empty carriage compartment with two long seats facing each other. I shut the sliding door and pulled down the blinds so that it was a bit more private, and lay out straight on one of the seats. I slept as the train passed through the Alps.

I awoke at dawn and, at almost the same instant, a small group of Italian school girls and a Catholic nun walked into my compartment and sat down. The nun was obviously their teacher at some private school and they were on a day trip out together, and here was I laid out in my sleeping bag. I sat up and they giggled and soon they were singing songs together. I guess they were religious songs, due to the nun leading them, but they were all in Italian.

As the sun was rising, I was mesmerised by the amazing landscape. Little Mediterranean villages with their olive trees, their terraced hillsides, and their orange, terracotta-roofed houses, all so wonderfully Italian. I was like a little child in a sweet shop. It was all new. It was exciting. And it was happening all around me. And I had a window seat!

The teenagers and the nun got off at some little station before my stop. I waved goodbye.

Soon after, the sea came into sight. I was on the Med!

I went and found the local youth hostel and booked in for a couple of nights. The building was like an old castle nestled on a hill overlooking the sea. Perfect. I lazed around the hostel, revelling in the scenic views across the Mediterranean.

A definite improvement on the previous night of bushes and dog dirt.

These new experiences and sights were making me giddy with excitement and I loved this new lifestyle that I was stepping into.

A couple of days later I was back on a train. It followed the north west Italian coastline south. Beautiful journey. My destination was a place called Pisa. It wasn't until I nearly arrived, that it dawned on me, 'Oh Pisa, leaning tower!'

So when I arrived, I had a mission of course. It wasn't long before I saw it. Walked to it. And climbed it! The view was good. The town was Italian! I was in Italy!

Come on! I like this life. So much to see, so much to explore. All so new. To me of course, not to the Italians!

Next stop Florence. Spent a day or two walking around looking at buildings and art. All very grand looking, but not so much my scene. Sorry Florence!

As I was looking at the map of Italy, I suddenly saw a place I recognised the name of and thought, 'Oh yeah, that's in Italy isn't it? I can't pass through Italy and not go there, even though it means going north and not south.'

I would go out of my way and indeed wander, now that I had the freedom, to do so.

On to... Venice.

It was about 160 miles from Florence, but, it was going to be worth it.

I arrived at Venice train station around lunchtime and spent the afternoon wandering the meandering alleys of Venice. The place was alive with photo potential, but I didn't squander my time pandering to it. Instead I rushed around exploring all the hidden nooks and crannies like an excited boy in an enchanted land.

Of course, I ended up in St Mark's Square with its famous church tower as I guess everyone who visits Venice does.

But I preferred the narrow alleys and little bridges over the canals as they were more secret and hidden.

When the sun started getting low in the sky I began thinking about where I could sleep rough. After getting a big bottle of mineral water and some food I decided to get out of the town and take a boat to an offshore island where there were a lot less people. On the island, I found a quiet sandy beach with some beach huts and not all of them were locked, which was good for me!

I cleaned the place up a bit and made myself at home. As I settled down for the night and things became still, alarmingly, my skin started coming out in a fierce rash and I began getting a fever, then shortly after, I started vomiting and having diarrhoea.

I was in a right mess. Fortunately, I had a deserted beach to be ill on.

Then very surreally, a massive beautiful firework display started up nearby for some grand occasion. I don't mean that my sickness was grand in the big scheme of things, but it was a nice gesture all the same! To be honest though, the sickness stole the show for me; the fireworks didn't get a look in.

Who needs a firework display when you can be sick, have a rash, fever and diarrhoea all at the same time?!

Anyway, it all eventually came out and I managed to get to sleep. I was exhausted.

The next morning, I just drank my mineral water and got on the first boat back to the mainland of Venice. Soon after disembarking the boat I started feeling hot and sick again and the rash was returning on my arms and stomach. I needed to find a hospital quick. I was not sure I was going to even make it, as I was getting weaker by the minute and feeling faint.

People directed me to the hospital and I was allowed to see the doctor immediately. It was good to be safe in a hospital sitting down. The doctor did some tests and looked at my rash. He said it was the sun and the heat, and gave me an injection of some sort.

His diagnosis was wrong, as I found out later!

But one thing was for sure, I needed to find a quiet and safe place to recover.

I looked on my map of Italy and located what looked like a quiet town in the Tuscany area of Italy. The town was called Arezzo and there was a youth hostel there. So, I got on a train and started travelling South again. The trip was about 200 miles.

I arrived before dark and decided to treat myself to a meal in a local restaurant. I didn't want to stir the sick beast again, but at the same time, I was hungry. I had slept well on the train and was stronger, although still delicate.

I ordered a simple meal and just drank mineral water.

After eating I made my way to the youth hostel in the centre of the town. It was a picturesque neighbourhood and I was glad to be there.

Soon after booking a couple of nights at the hostel, I made my way to the sleeping dorm. There were two other guys in the dorm and as we were chatting I started to feel sick again. The two guys in the room were concerned when I lifted my shirt to show them the rash, and when they looked at the skin on my back they said, 'The rash is literally moving up your back as we watch.'

I lay down on my bed and we turned the light off but kept talking.

One of the guys was an ambulance driver in America and he was telling me about allergies that people seem to have and that it can be hard to find out what the problem is. He was suggesting that I may need to go back to England and sort it out. I thought, 'NO, that's the last thing I want to do, I'm on the road.'

As I lay there, thinking what the heck should I do, I started to quietly contemplate what may have triggered the reaction in my body.

Then all of a sudden, the common denominator fell into my mind. I called out to the two guys in the stillness of the moment, while they were still awake, 'I know what it is!'

They said, 'What is it?'

And I replied with confidence, 'Mineral water.'

The sickness had started in the beach hut when I drank my bottle of mineral water and it happened again in the morning when I drank from the same bottle.

Then in the restaurant in Arezzo I had drunk Italian mineral water again.

I knew it was the problem and I was happy, because now I would not have to return to England and go through lots of allergy tests. Which come to think about it would not have helped, unless they tested me with that particular brand of Italian mineral water, which of course they wouldn't.

So, from that point on I was only going to drink tap water or water coming fresh out of a natural spring.

That is what I did. And the sickness never recurred.

After a couple of days recovery in Arezzo, enjoying the Tuscany countryside, I moved on south by train to Rome. Rome was busy and I remember car horns being honked on a fairly continual basis. Must be some kind of hobby!

I visited the basilica of St. Peter in the Vatican. As I entered the basilica there were hundreds of tourists and I felt insignificant, and for some reason decided to put up my multi-coloured umbrella inside. It made me feel less insignificant, but I wasn't popular for doing it and security staff came and told me to put it down.

I remember reading an article in an English newspaper once that was written by a headmaster of a school in London. He was commenting on why some people, especially teens, dress very outrageously. He used a phase that he thought may explain the phenomenon:

I cause attention therefore I am.

Maybe that's why I felt the need to put my umbrella up inside that busy building in Rome.

I ventured deeper into the Vatican territory and walked some of its plush corridors, eventually ending up in the impressive Sistine Chapel with its depiction of 'The Last Judgement' by Michelangelo painted on the ceiling. I remember my neck aching looking at it for a few minutes.

While I was in Rome I also had to visit the old Colosseum, because when in Rome... you do what the Romans... no sorry (that's wrong)... you do what the tourists do.

Things have changed there now, I have heard, but in 1985 when I went inside, the ruins were infested with stray cats. Hundreds of them. Cats and kittens everywhere.

Years later the authorities removed them all.

The authorities that were in power in Rome long ago did exactly the opposite. They deliberately let cats go into the Colosseum. The cats they let in were a lot bigger and wilder.

There was a reason for doing that, but it was not a good reason. Those bigger cats were called Lions.

After Rome, I travelled south to Naples. The further south I went, the more noticeable was the poverty. Naples was scruffier than the other cities I had visited, but I found it more alive and real.

In the back streets of Naples three kids were trying to sell neckties to people. They had piles of them. I had a laugh with them and tried in vain to explain that a tie was the last thing I needed in life. I was hardly doing office work!

Then I travelled to the ruins of Pompeii where Mount Vesuvius in A.D.79 had spewed its lava and caused so much death.

Even in this modern age Mount Vesuvius still dominates the landscape and is regarded as the most dangerous volcano in the world, due to the large population in its shadow.

In A.D.79 it covered Pompeii to a depth of five metres of volcanic ash, even with it being five miles away from the town.

The most spectacular part of Italy for me was to rear its head a bit later that week. It was the famous cliff top Amalfi coast road. Many films have used its backdrop and it certainly thrilled me with its beauty as I walked and hitched along its thirty miles of precarious, but stunning route from Salerno to Sorrento.

Every corner revealed a new scene, whether it was a lemon grove, terraced vineyard, Mediterranean villa, or the spectacular view of the winding road ahead cut into the cliff edge with the sparkling sea as it's backdrop.

Not far from the coastal town of Amalfi I came across some teenagers pulling up scrap fridges and ovens from a deep gully. People had dumped them off a bridge. These boys had a couple of Italian three-wheeler Piaggio Ape vans and they were lowering a rope down to their friend who was at the bottom of the chasm where the junk metal sat. He would then tie the rope to the fridge or oven and the guys at the top would attach the other end of the rope to the van and then they would drive along the road and pull the fridge up to the bridge. They then pulled it over onto the road and loaded it onto the back of the vans. I say vans, but they are more like scooters with a small van body on, with only one seat and steered by handlebars inside the tiny cab.

When they were both fully loaded and I mean fully, they pulled the boy up from the gulley and got ready to make their way to the local scrap merchant to get themselves some money. There were five boys and I asked if I could cadge a lift with them. It turned out that I was putting my life at risk, because here's the deal:

The van I squeezed myself into had no brakes at all!! It did however have a tiny engine (175cc), so it towed the other van with a rope... because that van had no engine... but it did have brakes. So, our van was only slowed down by waving to the guys we were towing and then they would apply their brakes, thus slowing us down. Our van pulled us up the hills and their van, slowed us going down the hills. Co-dependence!

It was a hairy trip.

When we reached Sorrento, I decided to find a place to sleep for the night and the next day I caught a boat to the island of Capri. I didn't see any poverty there, but I did see lots of big private residences tucked away behind their gates and walls! I spent the day walking around the area where all these *private castles* were, feeling quite empty and bored.

It was now time for me to leave the west coast and travel east to the port of Brindisi on the heel of the Italian peninsula.

Directly opposite Brindisi, across seventy-five miles of Adriatic Sea was the closed off nation of Albania.

My destination after Italy wasn't going to be Albania. Not that it could have been back then!

It was going to be Athens in Greece and after that, well maybe Israel, and then work on a kibbutz for a while. But I was beginning to have my doubts about that (which I'll explain shortly).

But before any of that, I was going to break my journey to Athens with a stopover on the island of Corfu. Why? Because the boat stopped there on the way to mainland Greece, so why not explore a bit?

I know the exact date I arrived at Brindisi to leave Italy for Corfu because something happened that evening causing the death of thirty-nine people and injuring six hundred others, most of them Italians.

It was the 29th May 1985. Liverpool and Juventus were in the European Cup Final. The match was being played at the Heysel Stadium in Brussels, Belgium. It was reported that one hour before kick-off Liverpool fans charged at Juventus fans in the stadium and the resulting chaos ended in the now infamous Heysel Stadium Disaster.

I was informed of this live scenario by some other travellers about my age who I met at the port that evening. There were reports that some angry people in Italy were beating English people up on the streets. There was a lot of tension around Brindisi that night as we waited for the ship to arrive. It was certainly a good time for an Englishman to be leaving Italy

The other travellers I met up with, who were also waiting for the same ship were all good to be around. We were all lone travellers from different parts of the world, who quickly struck up a rapport and ended up spending over a week together on Corfu.

I still remember most of their names: Paul from Hull in England, John from California, Ray from Australia, Steve from Canada, Mick from Australia and Mark from Torquay. (That was me, I always remember my name!)

It was Paul from Hull who had heard about the disaster taking place that night in Heysel Stadium and being the only two English guys around. We were keen to get on the ship and get away without being noticed.

We all had some bottles of wine between us and very soon, new friendships were blossoming.

When we boarded the ship, the crew onboard were listening to the live reports from the radio about the disaster. We could definitely feel the tension around us, but once the ship left port we all relaxed and drunk into the night on the deck under the stars. I was enjoying this new adventure with like-minded travellers and the next morning on our arrival in Corfu we all booked into the local youth hostel. We ended up sleeping on our bunks most of that day as we hadn't slept the night before, but over the next week we just hung out, chatted and got to know each other.

One particular chat with John from California ended up being instrumental in forming a concept in my mind that put me on a totally unexpected road of adventure.

I was telling John that I didn't fancy going to Israel anymore because it seemed that a lot of university students from around the world (especially from America) were travelling Europe with their *trusty travel booklets* in hand and many appeared to be on their way to Israel. To work on a kibbutz.

And that was not my scene; it was too safe, organised and predictable.

I needed to go somewhere that people were **not** travelling to.

Somewhere that was cheap and adventurous.

John said, 'What about Turkey? Not many people go there, and it's cheap!'

At that time, all I knew about Turkey was the film 'Midnight Express', which wasn't pleasant, but in that conversation with John, my interest in Turkey grew very quickly.

After travelling through Europe, I was also realising that places in themselves were not what it was all about. I would reach a destination and it was exciting for a while, but then it would become boring and I would think – where next?

And the new destination would become the place that was going to satisfy my life somehow. I was always chasing the rainbow and expecting the other end to reveal what life was all about.

I was always looking to something in the distance, rather than engaging with the present moment.

I needed to slow down and just walk, but there was a problem. I didn't want to carry my bag, it hindered my style. It was a necessary but unwanted burden.

Then as I was talking to John, things all fell into place in my mind and I said to him very definitely, 'I am going to go to Turkey and I'm going to buy a donkey, to carry my bag.'

And there it was. My future was laid out in front of me.

John and the other guys thought it was a great idea, and from then on I was hungry to find out anything I could about donkeys.

Later in the week, the six of us rented a moped each and went exploring the island of Corfu. I was the only one who was familiar with motorbikes, so it was second nature for me, but that wasn't the case for the others, as I was to find out.

Because it was so hot and the mopeds weren't exactly speed machines we didn't bother wearing helmets. We were young!

We rode up into the hills through small villages, stopping now and then at a viewpoint or local café.

On the way through the countryside the longest snake I have ever seen in the wild passed in front of me and it wasn't to be the last snake I saw that day!

We rode our mopeds up the long steep narrow dusty track that led to the highest peak on the island and when we reached the top we were treated to a clear view of Albania. Between there and Corfu was the short distance of sea in which many Albanians had tried to escape from the land of Communism to reach the land of Democracy. Many had died in their attempt. The eyes of the Albanian army were diligent in watching for such escapades.

Albania was the only country in the world which declared itself an atheist state and they didn't take kindly to their people leaving.

Albania was very unknown to the outside world at that time, as visitors were not allowed in, thus causing a stronghold of fear and mystery to surround it.

On the way back down the dusty track I saw my second snake of the day. I stopped to look at it, feeling safe on my moped even though the snake was only about six feet away from me. It knew I was there and started panicking to get away but couldn't get up the cliff right beside the track. Then all of a sudden it shot at my legs and I immediately lifted both of them and twisted the throttle to get away. I charged down the hill with my legs up in the air because I didn't know if the snake was caught up in the moped or maybe even my trousers! I don't really like snakes, especially venomous ones!

After riding full pelt with my legs high in the air, my thighs got cramp and I had to quickly stop, so I just braked, chucked the moped to the ground and ran away from it.

When I looked back and couldn't see the snake anywhere I returned to the bike, got on it, and got out of there.

Later on, more drama on the bikes was to occur when Ray from Australia totally misjudged a sharp corner in the hills and careered off the road, going through some vegetation and over a steep bank. When we scrambled down to where he was, we found him in a bloody mess and realised an ambulance was needed.

After what seemed like an age, one eventually turned up and it was a relief to see Ray taken away and in the hands of professionals.

The next day we were all to go our separate ways and I think maybe Mick from Australia eventually found out where Ray had ended up, but the rest of us never saw him again.

I stayed on the island a day longer than most of the other guys and boarded the ferry to the Greek mainland independently. I was on my own again... heading to Turkey to buy a donkey.

It had been a real fun time with the guys on Corfu and it was sad seeing us all go our separate ways, but the lifestyle I had chosen was to find out if I was a rock. Who was I, when I was on my own, away from friends, familiarity and security?

As I saw it, this was the road I needed to take if I was going to become a man of substance.

The ferry reached Patras in Greece and I caught a train that was on route to Athens via Corinth, passing over the impressive Corinth Canal gorge.

Once in Athens I booked in at the youth hostel, met up with other travellers from around the world and drank wine with many of them on the rooftop late into the night.

Again, I was with like-minded people and we discussed our different lives and dreams to each other. They loved the idea of my walking through Turkey with a donkey and I couldn't wait to get started.

I didn't bother walking up to the Acropolis while I was in Athens as everyone seemed to be going there and I didn't now want to get caught up in all the expectation of what people should do when in Athens. Seeing it from a distance was enough. I would get half the T-shirt and use it to wipe my brow, away from all the photographic frenzy.

I was slowly and subtly finding myself getting an appetite for wilderness existence.

I was soon back on a train and heading north, up through Greece – passing through such towns as Larnia and Larisa until I reached the large coastal port of Thessaloniki. In the local youth hostel I met a guy about my age from London called Richard who was into bird watching and had come to Greece on holiday for exactly that. The two of us got on well and met up in the evenings for supper.

One morning I went for a walk by myself down to the port area and saw a small crowd gathered around a guy with a large clipboard. He was English and had an interpreter working alongside him to translate what he was saying into Greek.

I didn't know fully what he was getting at, but then he started to say some interesting things and came to the bit where he said, 'Is your life just like going round a roundabout, working 9 to 5 every day, and life seeming monotonous and empty?'

I thought to myself, 'This guy is seeing life as I see it. So I became interested in what he was saying.'

Then he said something like, 'Well Jesus in the Bible said…'

At that point, I shut off and was out of there. He wasn't a cool dude at all. He must be a Christian.

I walked back to the youth hostel and met up with Richard. Somehow, I was not peaceful. Hearing about Bible stuff had got me niggled and I needed Richard to tell me it was all a load of rubbish. He impressed upon me that the whole idea of Christianity was indeed rubbish in his view and as for hell – how could that be true?!

Something had got under my skin down at the port when I heard the word Jesus and it made me feel uncomfortable. What if it was all true?

The next day I was feeling better and had just about shaken it off.

Richard was on his way to Alexandropoulos, the last coastal town in Eastern Greece, because the bird life around that area was good, apparently. And that was what he was into.

It was a one-hundred-and-fifty-mile journey and we ended up catching the train together as I was also going east to reach Turkey. We walked around Alexandropoulos for an hour and Richard pointed out some native birds in that area.

After saying our goodbyes, I headed north on a small train to the very northeast corner of Greece, following the adjacent Turkish border to my right.

At the end of the journey I was also quite close to the Bulgarian border. I found myself sitting alone at a remote outpost train stop wondering about my predicament of not having any Greek money left to make the short train journey to the Turkish border. Then a guy with blonde hair and a rucksack turned up. He was called Stefan and was from Sweden. He worked doing something with computers and had come to Greece for a walking holiday. He was on his way to Istanbul to get a flight back to Sweden.

Nowadays Turkey is a popular holiday resort, but back then it was fairly unknown to western travellers, so to see Stefan was quite a surprise and also a bonus, because he lent me some spare money for the train fare.

After the short train trip, we walked to the border post. It was quite intimidating as it was in a remote location and they had guns. Like I said earlier, all I knew about Turkey was the film 'Midnight Express'. And if you had seen that film and were walking into Turkey before it was a popular holiday destination, you also would have been nervous. We both made it through alive and proceeded to walk to the nearest town, which was Edirne.

It was a town that was living in the past by about thirty years. It was another world.

We booked in at a cheap hotel and the next day I was out on the streets to check how I could buy a donkey.

I found a travel shop with someone who spoke good English and he was prepared to go with me and look for a donkey to buy.

I definitely needed his help because English was not the language that all the people around me spoke!

It was a crazy day actually. People were very surprised to see me in their neighbourhood as I was dressed differently, had a scruffy look about me after being on the road for a while, plus I had a strange little beard and an earring in my left ear, which was not the 'done thing' in Turkey back then it seemed.

We ended up going out of town to a location where apparently a donkey would be available to buy. It was tied up at a building site and various onlookers became interested very quickly. Kids giggled at their new visitor and adults gathered and chattered about my interest in buying a donkey.

Then the owner arrived and paraded his donkey around for me, but it soon became apparent that it was totally blind!

So, because I wasn't starting a charity, I moved on.

I needed a donkey that could walk, and see!

Someone then told my helpful translator about another place to try and buy a donkey which ended up being the local gypsy community.

Now if I had an audience at the building site, I definitely had one at the gypsy camp, there were kids everywhere.

First guy like me who had wandered their way I bet.

I was glad to have the translator with me who could speak Turkish.

He was a smart well-dressed guy who didn't really fit in with the squalid conditions around us and I guess it was as much of a new experience for him as it was for me.

A female donkey, tied by the ankle to a post with a short bit of rope, was presented to us. She had a big hole through her nose that you could see through, which presumably resulted from some bad treatment with a stick.

She wasn't having a good life in that camp, let's put it that way!

Anyway, to cut a long story short, that was my donkey. I paid the equivalent of about thirty-five pounds for her and then proceeded to walk her back into town. You can imagine the attention I got. It was a crazy day in my life!

The little hotel I was staying at let me tie her to a post out in their backyard.

Stefan from Sweden was also still around and he decided that he would like to walk with me for the first couple of days before he moved on by bus to Istanbul.

The next day I went around the marketplace looking for things that I would need in order to survive, on the road and in the wilderness with a donkey.

I already had a sleeping bag but I had no tent or anything to sleep under. So I bought a three meter long sheet of cloudy transparent plastic which ended up being two layers thick, because when I opened it up, I found it was also joined at the edges. It was in fact a tube of plastic sheet that had been squashed flat.

This was perfect because I could then run a thin rope through the middle of it, tying one end to a tree and fix the other end to the ground somehow. To form a triangle entrance I would place two rocks inside to the left and to the right.

The other end I would just fold up and seal on the ground.

I bought an old sack and some wooden clothes pegs to create a door at the triangle entrance near where my head would lay each night.

I had been given an old traditional wooden saddle when I bought the donkey, so that was going to be useful to attach all my gear to as we walked together.

I bought a large wicker laundry basket with a lid, to tie to one side of the saddle and I hung my bag on the other side to balance the weight out.

The only map of Turkey I could get hold of seemed to indicate that much of the landscape was made up of mountains and desert scrub land, so not knowing where and when water would be available I bought two large plastic water containers.

I also bought some cheap kitchen utensils and a metal saucepan to put on a fire and cook with when I was in the countryside.

It was another crazy day and it was very useful having Stefan around to help me gather the things I would need.

The following day we were ready to leave.

The crowd of people that gathered around us, speaking and laughing in a foreign language as we struggled to arrange the load and set off, was not really what we needed, but eventually we made our way out of Edirne and the crowd slowly faded away.

The road southeast to Istanbul was the next scene of activity to negotiate, with lorries and cars rushing by and honking their horns, as they caught sight of us struggling along the roadside. We stood out like three sore thumbs!

The walk from Edirne to Istanbul was going to take me about two weeks as it was over one hundred and fifty miles and walking with a donkey was not easy, as I was quickly finding out. I was pulling her with a thin rope and she was resisting nearly all of the time. It's comical looking back, but at the time it was frustrating and a test of my patience.

As the sun was getting low in the sky at the end of our first day of walking, Stefan and I looked about to see where we could get off the road and hide from view, to set up camp for the night. We were exhausted.

We followed a small track that led off the road, set up the handmade plastic tube tent for the night and fell asleep very quickly. After about an hour or so we were woken by car headlights shining in at us. We were obviously worried about who it could be and as we got out of the tent, there in front of us were two men, one with a rifle in his hands!

We had no language to share but it was obvious that they wanted us off their land... sooner rather than later.

We hurriedly packed up all our stuff and wearily loaded it all back onto the donkey in no ordered way. In the pitch black, we disappeared off into the distance and eventually set up again, this time in a field by a little stream. Although apprehensive, we did manage to get to sleep again. What a first night!

In the morning, we got out of the tent to be welcomed by a rising sun and the sight of an old goat shepherd guy who was hovering about in our vicinity. As I wandered about to wake up a bit I was treated with the sight of something I had never seen before. The stream next to us was teaming with terrapins. Little aquatic tortoises everywhere. Loved it.

We set off onto the main road again for another hot day in the sun pulling a donkey. Stefan said, 'What are you going to call her?'

'Oh, I suppose I could give her name,' I thought, but first I needed to gauge her character a bit, so I didn't rush into it.

About half way through the day we came across a group of people all dressed in white and red T-shirts and caps. Also, the whole area where they were assembled was decked out in red and white bunting. There was some kind of promotional event going on and they were employees of the largest national newspaper in Turkey, 'Hurriyet'.

It wasn't long before they decided they wanted to interview us, (even though they didn't properly understand us!) so they took some photos, asked simple questions and promised to put an article in the national newspaper the next day.

 We bought a copy of the paper the next day and sure enough, it featured an article on Stefan, me and my donkey, including a colour photo of the three of us. When I got the article translated weeks later it turned out to be incorrect on many points. But hey!! Here today, gone tomorrow! All the bunting back in the box!

Stefan continued to walk with me another day and then went on his way to Istanbul by bus, to catch his flight back to Sweden.

I felt more vulnerable on my own, especially in the evenings when I had to look for places to hide from people before I could set up camp. It was a continual concern.

Walking from sunrise to sunset was pretty tiring, alongside the persistent, full on attention from nearly every Turkish person who set eyes on me. When I entered a town or village, I had to be sharp and alert until I exited. Exhausting!

An hour or so before sunset I would be on the lookout for places to hide, so being in the rural areas was a lot more suitable. If people knew where I was camping I would not be able to relax, because every few minutes people would be turning up and hanging around – not what I needed after a long, hot and dusty day on the road.

But, being vulnerable was what I was hoping to explore, to find out more about myself. My reasoning was that I was never going to fly, if I stayed in a safe comfy nest all my life.

Some late afternoons it was inevitable that I would be in the vicinity of humans before sunset. When that happened, I would indicate by hand signals that I needed a place to sleep in my tent. That would sometimes result in being shown someone's backyard, and then food was also offered to me. Which was all very nice, but in the bargain I would lose my privacy.

It was impossible to be left alone in that situation and difficult with no communicating language to answer everyone's curiosity as to who I was, where I was from and what I was doing walking with a donkey.

I was a total enigma to nearly everyone I met.

By the way, I gave the donkey a name! I felt her character deserved the name of Sophie. Of course, it wasn't 'Sophie's Choice'! ☺

I don't think I ever remember seeing Sophie actually sleep. I guess she must have because she was walking every day, usually from sunrise to sunset, but she did her sleeping out of sight from me, presumably when I was fast asleep! But even when I got up in the morning, there she was on her feet, usually eating grass or whatever was tasty and within her reach.

My own personal food which I put in the basket hanging from Sophie's saddle was usually a basic diet of bread, cheese, fruit and whatever else was being sold by the side of the road.

My water supply was from natural springs that I would often find on route.

One regular food was the supply of big green watermelons, which were always being sold by the road, and it was not just me who benefited from the purchase, because one of Sophie's favourite treats it seemed was watermelon peel. So, I would eat the red fruit inside and afterwards give Sophie the thick green peel to eat. It was a good arrangement we had.

I would also eat a fair bit of real Turkish Delight whenever I could get my hands on it. It was quite addictive and it kept my sugar levels up, which I needed.

Sophie wasn't involved with the Turkish Delight treat. Sorry!

As I walked each day I thought about so many things; goes without saying! I thought about friends and family back in England and how they would have no idea where I was or what I was doing. (There was no internet or mobile phones back then.) Most of the people I knew back in England had no idea even what country I was in.

My thoughts would rumble through the many situations that had happened in my life, happy and bad.

Walking on my own with a donkey forced me to be very contemplative and this was helped along by the language barrier I had with the people around me. I was never really having conversations, apart from the odd courteous exchange and friendly banter, which I didn't understand anyway.

So, I did a lot of thinking. It was a privilege really because it helped me process my life, and work through it in my mind. I had never had the luxury of such an extended period of time by myself. Some people of course would not find being on their own for a long length of time a luxury, but for me it was.

Don't get me wrong, it was also at times lonely, but within that, I could explore what I really thought about life.

My favourite place to sleep at night was in woodland. No one was likely to come across my whereabouts once I tucked myself away in the trees out of sight. I could relax better then.

Bears still roam around in Turkey, but when I heard strange noises in the depths of the night my reasoning usually was that they would probably attack and eat Sophie before me, thus giving me the opportunity to escape.

Sorry Sophie – you know it makes sense!

Anyway, maybe donkeys kick bears.

After about a week, the sea of Marmara came into view in the far distance and it was proof, by looking at my map, that I was now nearer to Istanbul than to Edirne.

Pulling Sophie along was a battle of wills and I don't know who was struggling more. My tactics had changed and I had tied the pulling rope to a foot long piece of wood, which gave me a type of handle to hold onto with both hands and this prevented me having to pull on the bare rope, but still my hands suffered.

Occasionally I would attempt to speed her up by walking behind her and clipping her backside with the stick. This worked to a certain extent but she had a cunning plot to ambush the procedure. She would veer off into the road, forcing me to rush in front of her to steer her back onto the dusty verge.

It was a clever plan that basically stalled the whole walking process, which was her ultimate goal and if the road was busy her plan always worked, because I had a brain which considered safety.

She didn't, she was a donkey.

So, it was a slow affair.

Many years later I read Robert Louis Stevenson's auto biographical book 'Travels with a donkey in the Cevennes'.

At one point in the book I laughed till I cried. There was a man who understood. We had walked the same road, so to speak!

Later in the journey I found an improved technique to control Sophie, but unfortunately, it was a while before someone showed me this.

My 25th birthday was the following week and it looked like it was going to be spent in Istanbul. It wasn't planned, but it was a good landmark for my memory.

As I got nearer to the city and its outskirts, the busier things were, both people and buildings. I couldn't do a thing about it. I was in it, so I had to suck it up.

Amazingly I managed to find a shoddy camp site of sorts. It was pretty basic, but it ended up being a very suitable place for me because it meant that I could put my plastic tent up and leave Sophie and my belongings on site while I went and investigated this oriental city of legends. I say oriental because it is where Europe ends and Asia begins. The Bosporus being the dividing line between the two. And indeed, the influence of the cultural marriage was evident in the architecture, the clothes, the markets, and the art.

I was camped quite close to the famous Blue Mosque. It was on my walking route to the hectic waterfront area of Istanbul. I carefully researched how I was going to walk into the city with Sophie and get on a boat across the Bosporus with as little hassle as possible. Not easy, with hundreds of potential inquisitors on my route. On this day, I was without Sophie. She was happily back at the campsite eating grass to her heart's content. She probably couldn't believe her luck.

And I was happy because I could go fairly incognito around the city and explore the place to *my* heart's content.

So, we were both happy. But I had more reason to be happy because it was my birthday. Although I was with no-one who knew, so it was quite a private affair!

I spent a few hours wandering the streets and the famous Istanbul bazaar. Plenty of salesmen there. In one shop, I spotted a good looking western traveller who looked like she had been on the road for quite a while. I had not really had a proper conversation with someone who spoke English for a couple of weeks and I could have done with some company.

And I quite fancied the look of this girl, so I plucked up the courage to go and ask her if she wanted to go for a coffee.

She said no. (I like to think she already had a boyfriend!)

Bit of a disappointment on my birthday, but I got over it. If anything had materialised, it would have stepped on the toes of my mission to find out who I was, by travelling alone.

But sometimes it's easier to jump into company and avoid the ache attached to emotional self-sufficiency. It's good she said no. I needed to be on my own. I still had untapped things to find out about myself.

The next day I loaded Sophie up and got myself ready to leave the campsite. When I say campsite, don't picture a bar, café, restaurant, marked camping pitches and other such amenities. It was an area of grass scrub land that was fenced off and had a gate. But it was suitable for my needs because it had a guard, water and a long drop toilet and I had no complaints, it had served me well. The morning I left, a wild tortoise was eating near my tent. I say wild, not meaning loose and dangerous, but meaning it wasn't someone's pet!

As I left the camp-site, my main concern was to get on the car ferry and across the Bosporus as quickly as possible, causing as little attention as possible. It was about a two mile walk to get to the ferry, and by the time I got there a small crowd had already latched itself onto me. When the ferry reached dock, I was pleased to walk on and lose them, but as the ferry was getting loaded with cars, a new crowd gathered around me. This time it was ferry passengers. It was the lorry drivers that were particularly interested in finding out about me and Sophie, but again, no common language.

The ferry floor was made of smooth metal and Sophie was extremely wary of this new type of ground.

I had paid someone in Edirne to nail small metal horse shoes to her feet. It was going to be a lot of walking and she needed good shoes. But these metal shoes were sliding on the car ferry floor and Sophie was not relaxed one bit. Then the unthinkable happened: all of a sudden her four legs went from under her and her belly hit the floor. She was helpless. All loaded up and four legs splayed out in a star position!

It sounds funny now, but for me then, it wasn't funny. I was very concerned.

The lorry drivers loved it. It was their entertainment for the day. More people gathered round and I was at a loss about what to do.

Then some of the drivers tried to lift her up. One guy was using her tail as a handle and I was outraged at this because I thought it was hurting her, but the guys gestured to me that it was fine. At this point we had reached the other side of the Bosporus and cars were driving off, but Sophie remained on the floor. Every time she was lifted up, she wouldn't stiffen her legs and stand by herself, because she didn't want to walk on that metal again.

It was a bit like when a toddler refuses to straighten its legs to stand up by itself when it is upset, it just collapses to the floor as soon as the parent stops lifting it.

In the end four lorry drivers literally lifted her and her load all the way off the ferry and onto the concrete ramp by the shore!

We were in Asia. Sophie was back on safe ground.

I had decided to walk in a north east direction to the coast of the Black Sea and it was going to take a few days but I wasn't constricted by time. I had all the time in the world.

It was good to get out of the hustle and bustle of Istanbul. After a few hours, I was on the open road again and the road to the coastal town of Sile was a lot quieter than the road from Edirne to Istanbul. And that's the way I liked it; time to think and watch the beauty around me unfold. Walking slowly made me very attentive to the environment around me and engage with the present moment, rather than always chasing the future horizon of hypothetical contentment.

The satisfaction, the fulfilment... the answer even! It had to be in the now.

I was living my dream and I was going to explore and enjoy it as much as I possibly could. There was so much to take in. If my friends back home could *only* see me now... but of course... they couldn't.

So, it was for me to see... and me alone.

I was finding hidden places to sleep each night and had even got into lighting a small fire and boiling a few vegetables in my saucepan.

After a few days, I arrived on the sleepy outskirts of Sile, an hour or so before sunset. The Black Sea was down below me with its picturesque old fort on a rocky outcrop. It was idyllic to the eye. A secret paradise at the end of the trail, but to fully enjoy this paradise, I first had to find myself a quiet and safe location to set up camp.

As I was overlooking the town, two young Turkish guys in their late teens arrived on the scene. They couldn't speak any English, but were as usual very intrigued and excited about having a foreigner with a donkey in their neck of the woods. I didn't want them around to be honest, because to have a safe place to sleep I needed no one to know where I was. So I was in a predicament. I couldn't just disappear from their view, because they were following right along beside me; plus to make matters worse, they seemed to have a streak of mischievousness about them, but I was stuck with them. It was slowly starting to get dark and I needed to put my plastic up and get things sorted out before I lost the light.

Begrudgingly, I found a patch of land and started to unpack. The guys wanted to help and I made it clear I didn't want them around my stuff, so they stood a few metres back from me by the tree that I had tied Sophie too. Meanwhile I started putting the plastic tent up.

I had already taken the wooden saddle off and was using it as an anchor-point for the end of the tent rope. All the time I was wondering how this awkward situation would resolve; there was a very real danger now that word would get out that a foreign stranger was in town with a donkey. And that was food for the masses.

I had already found that out a couple of times on the journey so far. One incident in the early days of my walk: I had had a whole village surround me in the evening and not let me out of their sight. They were caught in a frenzy of interest. They just hadn't seen the likes of it before and it was exhausting trying to respond to everyone's curiosity, in a language they didn't understand one little bit, and of course I couldn't understand their questions either!

As I was contemplating my present dilemma I could hear the two boys getting louder and one was giggling.

So, I turned around to see what they were up too.

Now if you're squeamish, maybe close your eyes at this bit.

I wish my eyes had been closed, but they weren't.

One of the boys had his trousers and pants halfway down his legs and was lifting Sophie's tail and was having intercourse with her.

Now I realise that is shocking to read, but imagine what it was like for me, being there! I was aghast.

I immediately started shouting at them. The guy with his trousers down extracted himself and started to pull his trousers up and then they started running off at half speed across some wasteland nearby. I ran after them still shouting as loud as I could to keep them wary of me. I chased them until they were out of sight, then I turned around and ran back to Sophie and the tent as fast as I could. There was no way I was going to stay camped where I was now. Those two guys would be back with a load of mates in the night.

By the time I had packed everything away and was ready to move on, it was completely dark. I was very shaken up by the whole incident and wished I had a mate with me to help make sense of it all. A mate who would agree with me that what had just happened was out of order. But I was stuck with being the minority in that opinion, being outnumbered two to one. Those guys didn't see anything strange in what they were doing with a donkey.

I was on my own and I was out of my comfort zone but, 'I had made my bed and I had to sleep in it.'

Making my physical bed was the immediate priority right then too, because I was very tired after the long days walk. This incident and the accelerated adrenalin had just about finished me off.

I rushed from the scene as quick as I could in the near darkness and had no idea where I was going or what I was going to do, but I needed to get as far away from that place as possible.

I think I walked hurriedly for about half an hour into the night and found myself, who knows where?

I skirted around the town through fields I think and ended up just forcing myself and Sophie through a thicket and down into a dry ditch. I didn't even put the tent up. I just huddled into my sleeping bag and was grateful to be away from people's awareness of where I was. I slept deeply. I think.

The next morning, very early, before the sun had risen, I got the hell out of that place and all things to do with it.

The 'rock' that I had hoped I was, had revealed a fault line.

I was finding things out about vulnerability. It had been a rude awakening. The top layer of skin had now been removed. Paradise lost.

In one sense the drama had turned out for good, because it had resulted in getting the two boys out of my space.

I think it would have been a longer ordeal if the incident hadn't have happened, because they would have hung around into the evening and I'm not sure how I would have got rid of them and relaxed afterwards, knowing that they and others would probably return after I had gone to sleep.

But emotionally, it had still taken its toll on me.

From the outskirts of Sile I started to make my way to the coastline of the Black Sea – but further east.

After an hour or two, I found myself on a sandy shoreline in a remote area with no one around at all and the Black Sea lapping at my feet. No people, no road and no buildings. Maybe paradise hadn't been lost after all.

Sophie all loaded up, walking along the coastline of the Black Sea

I walked along that sand on my own for most of the day. Of course, Sophie was with me, but you know what I mean. As far as Sophie was concerned, I think the sand and sea must have been a totally new experience for her. Very different from her experience in the gypsy camp, tied to a post a hundred miles from any sea.

Walking through the sand out in this remote location right next to the sea, although slow going, was very therapeutic to my soul. It was certainly a welcome tonic from what had happened the previous day.

Yet even around such beautiful scenery a niggling thing kept popping it's head up in my thoughts as I walked along each day; it was the sentence that my old boss from 'Small Woodlands' said to me before I left England, 'As long as you know why you are travelling, because it seems to me that a lot of people who travel, are lost souls.'

It was that *lost soul* bit that niggled me. It implied that I didn't have it all together. That I was scrambling around in the dark through life. The words challenged my pride. They were an affront to my ego, and I didn't like it. I was out there living a real adventure. I was free. I wasn't stuck in some monotonous 9 to 5 job, with the shackles of a mortgage around me, or getting married and doing what the majority of people back home seemed to be doing.

However, I wrestled and reasoned in my mind. I couldn't get rid of those words: *lost soul*.

They were under my skin and a continual irritant.

There were also times I remember that I would sing a sentence out as I walked along on my own.

It was a question more than a sentence and my ego would never have admitted to anyone on earth that I needed to ask it. But the truth is that I did sing it out as I walked along with Sophie on my own.

The words I would sing out were: 'What's it all about – I really wanna know?'

I used the melody from the song by Rose Royce, where they sing the lines: 'I'm wishing on a star to follow where you are.'

When I sang those words: 'What's it all about – I really wanna know?', they really came from somewhere deep in me and the sentiment was: what the heck is life all about?

Usually there were plenty of distractions going on in the day, which alleviated me from singing or thinking it all the time!

But spending time on my own was searching me out. I left England because I wanted to find out what was real. I was searching for something better and my logic was telling me that it was 'out there' somewhere!

And here I was... out there!

But when I was 'out there', I found myself singing that song!

Oh well, better keep walking. Got nothing else do.

After a few days of walking along the southern shore of the Black Sea coast, I perused the basic map that I had got for free back in Edirne. I didn't have any destination as such, I was just heading in an easterly direction. Maybe one day I would end up reaching Mount Ararat by the eastern border of Turkey and cross over into Iran or something, but there was a long way to go before I would have to make that decision, so I just headed generally east.

As I looked at the map I saw a road running parallel to where I was walking on the coast, it was south of where I was and there were about forty miles of woodland between me and it. I reckoned I could find some sort of track going over the hills and come out the other side and join the road somewhere along its route. There were no tracks through the hills marked on my map... but I thought, 'Hey, let's go for it.'

As I turned inland from the coast I did find a track that I thought would head me in the right direction.

It was fun to explore and find my own way through the geography of the land and it was peaceful going through the hills. Occasionally I would come across a remote village and the people I came across were definitely shocked to see me walk through. They couldn't believe their eyes. Kids were going crazy with excitement and gathering around. Then the adults came asking more questions which I couldn't understand. Then on down the track until I reached the next community.

On my second day in the hills and not long before sunset I found myself in the company of two young teenagers. They had appeared out of the woods and were following alongside of me asking questions in Turkish. One of the boys was quite annoying. Maybe he was frustrated not knowing who I was, maybe he wanted something from me.

Maybe both and maybe neither.

To be honest, I can't remember the reason why he was annoying, but he was distinctly different from the other boy.

In the rural areas, I would sometimes come across individuals that were troubled. I want to choose my words here... I would see some slightly warped personalities. Some of them were really quite strange.

This boy was more like a bluebottle fly buzzing about in my room and he didn't want to leave the room, which was unfortunate for me because I needed him out of my room before I could attempt to find somewhere safe to set up camp.

After a while we reached a cluster of houses and the boy appeared to live in or around that area. I didn't want him to know I was looking for a place to sleep so I just walked onto the property of one of the rural houses there and hoped he wouldn't follow me. He didn't follow but he was nearby watching. I knocked at the door of the house and an old man came to the door. I indicated to him that I needed to set a tent up for one night and pointed to the hazelnut orchard on the hill by his house. He knew what I wanted and eventually led me up into the orchard with the small trees. I picked a place halfway up the hill, well away from the house and that night I went to sleep easily as usual, due to a full day of walking under a hot sun.

Sometime after midnight I awoke to voices outside my plastic tent. It was quite disconcerting to be woken by strange foreign voices at this time of night and I could tell from their tone that there was mischief in the air.

I begrudgingly appeared out of the tent entrance and there were about seven teenagers waiting to see the strange visitor. They were having fun, at my expense.

It was an intimidating time and there was not a thing I could do about it.

All the usual fragmented forms of communication went on, which was exhausting, especially in the middle of the night.

I think they were there for about an hour. I was on edge all the time and probably they knew it, because it was obvious I needed to get to bed. I thought they were going to be there all night but eventually they went off, leaving me very tired and also shook up.

I was definitely finding out I wasn't a *rock*.

My resources were crumbling. I was vulnerable and those guys picked up on it.

My main concern during the journey on the road was, whether I would get a safe place to sleep at the end of each day, and the fact that I had no easy way of escaping dodgy situations brought with it an added concern.

I was on foot, with my belongings and a donkey. Sophie was definitely not an escape vehicle for me, she couldn't even walk as fast as me!

When the sun rose the next morning, I was weary after my broken night. I packed up the gear and put it on Sophie. After I left the property, the guys turned up again and I recognised one of them as the annoying boy from the day before, on the road.

It must have been him who lined up the invasion in the night. He still had issues with me, but now he had his older mates. He started shouting at me as I walked along and then he started throwing stones at me and Sophie. He was mostly missing us, and eventually I was around the corner and on my own. But I was also aware that word gets around those hills quickly and I was still in the hills, so it was hard to relax.

It was not the last time I would have stones thrown at me. Later in the journey a shepherd boy got angry because I wasn't talking his language and threw stones hard at us, one of them hit Sophie in the head and blood started coming out.

But like I said before, I couldn't quickly escape these situations.

As I walked through the hills I passed remote communities and there seemed to be no more repercussions arising from the incident in the morning, but it did not alleviate my fears concerning safety at night. It had become quite an issue in my mind because I never knew where I would sleep each night, until I got there.

My mind also started seriously thinking about my whole situation in Turkey. I had walked over three hundred miles, but I was still only about a quarter of the way across Turkey.

I had been walking for about a month and I had a three-month visa, that could only be renewed back in Istanbul or Ankara. If I kept walking east towards Mount Ararat I would not reach the Iranian border before my visa ran out.

That meant I would have to leave Sophie somewhere in eastern Turkey then get a lift all the way back to Istanbul or Ankara to renew my visa, then return to Sophie and continue the walk east again.

It was a demoralising thought that sucked the life out of me.

I was getting depressed and anxious very quickly.

I was also fully aware that even if I needed to go back to England straight away, I couldn't, because I was in the middle of nowhere.

It was unnerving to know that I couldn't quickly escape, if the need arose.

Both those thoughts started to crowd in on me.

I was vulnerable and quite fearful. 'What the heck am I doing?'

As I walked along with these thoughts in my head, I blurted out, 'God, are you real? Are you there?'

Then, as I was saying it, I started to think I was going mad and pulled myself together again.

I was all over the place. I was wobbling. I was on shaky ground.

An hour or so before sunset I reached the road going east that I had set off from the coast to look for two days earlier. I had made it through the remote woodland hills. My navigation skills had worked well.

Next job was to find somewhere safe to camp for the night.

I decided that I would knock at the door of a house and ask if I could camp in their yard. The owner and his family let me. So, most of the evening was spent trying to answer all their questions. And again, the language barrier. I tried hard. They were being hospitable. But I would have preferred to just be on my own and relax.

The next morning, I expressed thanks and went on my way.

My walk now followed a tarmac road, just north of a town called Bolu. The road was busy with beaten up old lorries, and of course cars. But it was the lorries I mainly noticed because the drivers would often honk their horn when they passed me. Which I could have done without really!

About halfway through the day I was on a fairly quiet stretch of road and I was still not feeling too buoyant about life, but was just getting on with it. Then in the distance I heard someone shouting from a house to my left and off the road a bit.

He came running over to me saying, 'Hello, hello'. As he approached me I realised he could speak English. I still remember his name! He was called Semi.

Semi was excited to talk to me and insisted on me coming to his house to chat and tell him who I was and what I was doing. He was Turkish but had been living in Australia for many years. He was visiting Turkey for a couple of weeks and was hoping to buy some land in that neighbourhood.

He really was pleased to have met me and talk in English. It was the language he was used to using, of course, living in Australia.

Well that was great for me, because I needed to talk to someone in English too. I had not had a proper conversation with anyone for a month now, and to make matters even better, we got on well.

We talked about so many things. We were talking even as the evening set in. Semi offered me a place in the garden to put my tent up (I preferred sleeping outdoors), so I relaxed, knowing where I would sleep; and we continued talking, eating and drinking. It was such a treat. I told him about some of my exploits and predicaments on the road. He was a good listener and tried to assure me that most people in Turkey would let me camp in their yards.

We talked about deeper things in life as well. At one point Semi asked me a strange question, he said, 'Mark, do you believe in God?'

I replied, 'Well it's funny you mention that because yesterday I actually started to call on him, but I stopped myself.'

Semi then insinuated that it is a bit strange to only think about God when I needed something. He suggested I try and balance it out a bit and say 'thank you' occasionally too.

It was quite a refreshing thought he had challenged me with. I could see the sense in his logic.

He never mentioned anything else about God. That was it!

After a full, stimulating day and evening of conversation I went out into the backyard, got into my tent and slept peacefully.

The next morning after breakfast Semi and I said our goodbyes and I set off along the road east again. It was sad to leave good company and after an hour or so of walking, I felt the impact of being on my own again.

As the morning went on I again started thinking about what I was doing in life.

I had seen travelling as the big lump of wood that would never sink. I somehow knew that other bits of wood were out there to try, but they did not stay afloat for long.

Those other bits would not satisfy; they would get boring, let me down and not be buoyant enough to keep me above water for the rest of my life.

Bits of wood like: close relationships, careers, possessions, hobbies, money, beauty, popularity, drugs, partying and other things that people occupy their lives with.

They didn't last, they didn't fill the gap for me. I was still fairly young and had only tasted a sample of these things, but I could see in other people's lives that they were not dependable bits of wood. Travelling was the big lump of wood that was never going to sink. It was never going to become boring, it would allow me to be free to do whatever I wanted, and whenever I wanted. It would continually surprise me with new things. It would always satisfy and fulfil me.

Trouble was, I was realising that that big lump of wood was also soaking up water, and was not as buoyant as I thought.

No-one else knew the adventure I was having. I was out there on my own. I was the only one living it.

If I was honest with myself (and I needed to be at least honest with myself), I had hit a wall and the wall was: the realisation that travelling wasn't meeting the needs in me that I thought it would.

What was I to do with that knowledge?

Go back to England and buzz around on my ego about all that I had done!

And then what?

Maybe go somewhere else in the world like South America and do it all again!

But... if I was being real with myself, I had to admit that I would eventually hit the same wall out in South America.

Alongside this realisation was the persistent and very real fact that I was walking east and would not be able to reach the eastern border before my visa ran out.

Every step I was taking with Sophie in that direction was becoming pointless and sapping motivation out of me.

I was seriously struggling.

Here I was out in the ocean, hanging onto a big lump of wood that was never going to sink. I had left the safety of land because land wasn't giving me the answer. I had believed that the answer was out there somewhere, and I needed to search for it on my own.

So here I was, on my own, trusting in this piece of wood to carry me into the answer of what Life was all about!

But it was sinking. Sinking very quickly in fact, whether I wanted to believe it or not.

I was at a loss of what to do as I started to go down into the cold seawater of reality.

Water started going into my mouth as I wrestled frantically with the fact that there was nothing else in the water to grab hold of.

All other forms of security were out of reach (hundreds of miles out of reach).

I never expected it would come to this. I was panicking. I was more scared than I had ever been in my whole life. I took another gulp of water into my lungs. There was nothing else in life that was going to do the trick.

I was not a rock... far from it!

My resources were spent... totally.

I was terrified.

There was nothing in this life that was real enough to meet my need.

Then I took the third and final gulp of water and as it went down into my lungs for the last time, I was brought face to face with the death blow: The futility of my existence.

As I was about to submerge totally under the surface and out of view, a cry for help erupted from the depths of my being.

It was a cry that had not been planned or even thought in my head, but still it came out of my mouth in words.

The words were: 'If you're there God, give me a direction in Turkey… give me a direction in life… and give me a purpose in life.'

Within a second of that coming out of my mouth – my attention was taken by a car passing me with a GB sticker on and English number plates. It was a Mercedes and was pulling off the road further up, parking on the dusty roadside.

I couldn't believe it.

I forgot about the prayer and what had been going on in my thoughts beforehand.

I was now focussed on reaching that car before it pulled away again. It was the first vehicle I had seen with English plates since I had been in Turkey.

A lady had got out of the passenger seat and walked to a building by the side of the road.

I started to pull Sophie, as I attempted to run.

When I reached the car, I knocked on the driver's window to get the attention of the slightly Turkish looking man sitting there. He looked at me and wound down his window. I said with a smile, 'Where are you from?'

He replied, 'London! Where are you from?'

'Torquay!'

He then got out of his car and carried on the conversation with, 'What are you doing out here with a donkey? We saw you walking along back there and thought you were a Turkish peasant.'

I informed him that I had bought the donkey in Edirne.

He was amazed that I had walked all the way from Edirne and enquired where I was going. I told him that I was thinking about Mount Ararat and the eastern border. He then said something that surprised me about Turkish people not particularly liking Christians, and Turkey being a hard land to be in for visitors

I was surprised by this passing comment from him and for a brief instant I remembered the prayer I had said a few minutes earlier. I couldn't help connecting the prayer, with this sudden mention of Christianity, from a stranger who had popped up out of apparently nowhere.

But it was a fleeting recognition in my head, that of course he was totally unaware of.

He then went on to say that I should not go any further east.

He told me that the country further east turns into a barren wasteland and that there were some people in that area who would not think twice about slitting my throat and hiding my body in the hills, just to get hold of my money and possessions.

He had been there and knew the area and was extremely serious with me. He said, 'Take it from a friend, don't go any further east!'

I said, 'Well it's funny you should say that, because I was wondering about my whole direction in Turkey and what I should be doing.'

At that point, his wife arrived on the scene. The man told her what I was doing and we chatted for a few more minutes together. Just before they got back in their car to leave, I said, 'Where are you two on your way to?'

And they replied, 'Mersin.'

I got my map out for them to show me where Mersin was. It was right down south by the Mediterranean Sea.

I had already walked nearly three hundred and fifty miles and the distance to Mersin was about another five hundred miles. So, if I walked at the same speed, I reckoned I could reach Mersin before my visa ran out.

Then I looked and saw Cyprus off the coast of southern Turkey.

I said to the couple, 'Wow... I could go to Cyprus!'

And the man said back to me, 'You could stay in Cyprus till doomsday!' He meant that I would not have any visa problems on Cyprus due to my British passport.

I made my mind up there and then that I would change my direction in Turkey and head south. And the crazy thing was, at the town a few miles ahead of me called Gerede there were just two main roads: the one I was on which continued east, and one branching off it which went south through the heartland of Turkey, until it reached the coast at Mersin.

The couple got back in their Mercedes to leave, shut their doors and kept their windows down to say goodbye. They kept looking me straight in the eyes with big smiles and the words they kept saying to me as they slowly pulled away were, 'God bless you, God bless you.'

And then they were gone.

I was left there by the side of the road in a fixated state.

God was flaming real. I knew without a shadow of a doubt that He was there with me.

He had heard my cry and answered immediately.

When I had been living back in England and got a bit depressed I can remember saying in my room once, 'God if you're there, move that chair a bit, so that I can see it move.'

If He was there I wanted to know!

I wasn't being arrogant, but even so, my intellect needed some proof!

Well, the chair never moved! So, I went on with life as normal.

But on that road in Turkey, my prayer had been desperate and had come from somewhere a lot deeper in me.

And God had responded to that cry for help.

He had immediately come and plucked me out of that deep water I was drowning in.

He had indeed given me a direction in Turkey. I was now about to go south, rather than east.

And now that I knew God existed, I had a direction in life and a purpose in life.

Of course, I didn't know what the new direction and purpose would look like, but the very fact that God was there, was enough.

He was the reason for direction and purpose. He had made me for a 'purpose', because that's what creators of anything do, create things for a purpose, else there is no point in creating anything.

'The futility of my existence' was no longer an issue.

And boy was I flaming happy!

It is quite hard to convey the emotions I went through by the side of the road that day. It was such a huge revelation to me that God was real. It was so exciting to know that life had a purpose, that it wasn't all an accident that floated about in the haze of chance.

All of a sudden, I had immense hope. The future was pregnant with adventure and meaning.

The gap that I had been trying to fill, had a reason for being there.

It was waiting to be filled with God and only God, I realised, He was big enough and real enough to fill it. Nothing else was ever going to do the trick! He was the exact size and shape to completely fill the empty void I had felt deep inside of me. There had always been something missing!

It now all made sense. He was the piece in the puzzle, that once in position, made the rest of the picture make sense.

It was no longer a secret or a mystery. The truth had been unveiled to me. It was certainly not found out by my supposed wisdom or cleverness!

I had to keep on walking, but in a sense, the wonder of it all could have kept me on that spot for days.

That would have got in the papers: *Man stuck on spot in 'state of wonder' by side of road in Turkey!*

So, I walked on, because life had taken on a whole new look.

I hope some of you have seen the film 'The Matrix'. The moment where Morpheus offers Neo the choice of the blue pill or the red pill.

If Neo takes the blue pill: his life will continue to be stuck in the illusion of reality and he won't ever be able to leave it.

If he takes the red pill: he will find out what real life is, and how deep the rabbit hole of reality goes.

I was off down that rabbit hole!

I reached the town of Gerede and branched off south towards Ankara.

Little did I know at the time, but as I turned south at Gerede I started entering a region mentioned in the Bible called Galatia. The letter to the Galatians, is one of the books written by Paul in the New Testament.

I was now following my new direction in Turkey.

As I walked I tried to recall things I knew about Christianity. I remembered the hymn 'All things bright and beautiful, the Lord God made them all', so I sang a couple of lines from that many times over. I also remembered that a friend called Karen from my biker days had told me that the group U2 were Christians. So I just sang the line 'In the name of Love' over and over again!

I also recalled most of the 'Lord's Prayer.'

It was all a bit basic, but it was all I had at the time.

I asked God to meet me up with a Christian and also to get me a Bible.

As it turned out, I had to wait quite a while for those two things to happen!

After about three weeks of walking south, I approached Tuz Golu, which was a big inland salt water lake. The city of Ankara was about one hundred miles behind me. I had walked around it, as I didn't need to enter into the chaos of a city.

The terrain I was walking in was semi-desert and very barren.

Then something started to happen to my leg muscles. They started seizing up. Within a few minutes I couldn't even walk. Obviously, this was very disconcerting, there were no buildings anywhere in sight, not even a tree to rest under and get shade.

I tried to get onto Sophie's back, but she didn't seem to be able to take my weight, so I gave up on that idea. Then as I strained my eyes I thought I could see a building in the very far distance. It gave me a reason to struggle on very slowly and after about half an hour I could see that it *was* a building. And half an hour after that I could make out that it was probably a fuel station.

When I eventually got there I was in a right mess. My stomach didn't feel good and I was feeling nauseous. The guy at the forecourt and some others were surprised to see me, but they could also see that I wasn't well.

The place was actually a trucker's rest stop. They tied Sophie to a post in the shade and indicated they would look after her. The guy then took me slowly up to a dorm room with about six beds in and I lay down. I ended up being in that bed for a few days. I was not well. I was sick and had dysentery. If that building had not been where it was, I don't know what I would have done.

There was a long drop toilet along the corridor that was quite basic, but boy was I glad it was there! And it was where I hung out for the first day or so. I was totally without energy for a few more days after that and I didn't even have an appetite. The guy popped up to see me once or twice a day to check I was alive, which was nice.

Slowly I started to get an appetite and ate some simple food he brought for me, but I was not fit to leave the building. So, I stayed and just read the only book I had, which I had bought in Corfu because it was in the English language. It was 'Death on the Nile' – the murder mystery by Agatha Christie (who was actually born in Torquay!)

I ended up reading it twice and was very grateful for the distraction it gave me whilst feeling weak and ill in that bare dormitory room.

Eventually I ventured out into the world of hot sun, Sophie and the garage forecourt. The day after that, I was ready to move on. The guy did not charge me for his hospitality, bless him.

Before I left I had a big omelette, because while I had been laid up, I had done some thinking about my leg muscles seizing up. All I really knew about muscles was that they needed protein and that was something that I hadn't been having much of.

So, from that day on I made sure I ate eggs whenever I could. Omelettes.

My legs never suffered like that again.

It was good to be on the road again and during that first day, I came into the vicinity of Lake Tuz (Tuz Golu) which is a forty mile long, inland salt lake. I had seen its waters glistening in the far-off distance when my legs had started seizing up a few days earlier, but now I was up close, I could appreciate its salty quality – especially along it's distinct white shoreline.

It was a very remote and barren area. It made me think to myself, 'I'm out here in the middle of nowhere in Turkey, and no one I know has a clue where I am or what I'm up to.'

It was a good feeling and very empowering in a way.

I felt quite proud of myself.

The barren terrain and salty deposits around lake Tuz
(in the region formerly known as Galatia)

My immediate destination, after leaving the safety of the truck-stop garage and dormitory, was a town called Sereflikochisar. It was a full day's walk to reach and I didn't pass any other dwelling places on route to it. My body was still weak after my prolonged illness, but I could also feel that it was getting stronger. My plan was to try and find a cheap but comfortable place to stay for two or three days and fully recover.

On entering the town there was immediate and frenzied interest in who I was and what I was doing in such a remote place. Of course there was still no common language, so it was hard for everyone, but especially me, as I was the odd one out!

I managed to book three nights in at some basic accommodation. It was good to be able to just stop, sort myself out, relax and be in a safe place for a few days. It was also nice to just walk about the town without Sophie. It made me a little bit more invisible and freed me up to wander about at my speed and not have to worry about keeping an eye on my belongings.

I treated myself to some nice simple meals at the local eating places. To be honest, simple was about all that was on offer anyway!

There was one job that had to be done in Sereflikochisar and for that I needed to find the local blacksmith. Sophie's metal shoes from Edirne had come to the end of their life.

I left Sereflikochisar feeling a lot better than when I had entered and hopefully so did Sophie, now she had her new shoes on.

Another thing to mention about my ongoing relationship with Sophie was that, I was now the boss. A couple of weeks earlier when I was in the north of the country, an old Turkish man had indicated for me to stop walking.

After a few minutes, he returned with a five-foot long wooden branch. It seemed that he had seen me struggling with Sophie and he had gone off and cut the long branch from a nearby tree. He then indicated that I should throw the little stick I had been using away. With the long branch I could now walk behind Sophie and use it to steer her, by flicking it near the side of her head when she attempted to veer off course. Also, I could clip her backside if she slowed down too much.

Oh, what a blessing that man was to me.

I could now proceed in a much more orderly fashion. It was so much easier.

I was now in control of the situation – I was the boss... at last!

I was good to be back on the road south again but there were still many miles to cover before I would leave the remote and barren landscape around me. There were not even trees or bushes to hide behind, which was what I needed in the evenings. So, my ongoing concern was where I would safely lay my head at the end of the day.

My experience with God over two hundred miles back had lost some of its intensity due to the ongoing struggles of the walk especially the time of sickness that I had been through. I had not bumped into a Christian or got hold of the Bible, which I had asked God for. Maybe He had a better idea, but as yet I wasn't seeing it.

The landscape I was walking in going south, continued to be almost devoid of trees, which wasn't helpful for my sleeping arrangements, as trees were very useful for tying my tent rope too and also for keeping me out of sight from inquisitive humans.

One particular late afternoon as I walked along this desolate landscape and my shadow was getting longer, I had still not seen a good place to stop, but in the distance, I could make out a small building. When I reached it, the owner was not really interested in helping me out with a camping spot.

But nearby there was a scruffy guy who had a shack where he mended tyres. It appeared that the man slept in the shack at nights and he indicated to me that he didn't mind that I also slept on the floor. It was a very small building that probably measured six foot by six foot. So, it was a squeeze! And it also was very hot in there because it was made of brick and situated in the sun. I can't remember there being a window either. It also smelt of tyre rubber and glue!

But it was safe and it was nice of that man to let me share his humble abode for a night. Bless him.

As the night progressed and the air outside got colder, the building slowly cooled down. So, luxury really.

On the last two days in that remote desert type region I walked about fifty miles and reached a town just after the sun had set. I really had to push hard to get that distance covered with Sophie, but seeing a town on the map further south made me determined to reach it in two days. It had been sunrise to sunset walking on both days.

I managed to get a room in a building that rented rooms out. It's a good job I did because that night I started feeling very cold and extremely weary. I think I was suffering from exhaustion after two days of stressful walking, on top of not being well before that. My body was just not getting warm. Amazingly there was a small wardrobe in the room and inside it were five blankets. Those five blankets were just enough to warm my body up and I fell into a deep sleep.

In the morning I felt refreshed and fully recovered. I had made it through the sickness and the semi-desert terrain. Things were looking good.

As I continued walking, the geography of the land started to change dramatically. I left the flat desert scrubland area and entered a mountainous region.

It was a good change that brought streams, rivers, bushes, trees, grass, bird-life, rich colours and different views to look at around each corner.

And with it a change in mood – as I walked in this southern part of the country I began to enjoy the prospect of reaching the Mediterranean Sea.

I remember one night in this particular stretch of the journey, sleeping on the flat roof of a building, in the hills. There was no light pollution in that region and the night stars filled my view as I lay contented on my back.

It's good to soak that stuff up now and then – does something for the soul.

As the days and miles were covered, I eventually started to near the famous town of Tarsus.

(I only found out it was famous months later though.)

Tarsus was the hometown of Saul from the Bible. You may have heard of Saul and his Damascus road conversion. It was where Jesus revealed himself very definitely to Saul (later called Paul) on the roadside. His God experience by the road, was a lot more full-on than mine (see the book of Acts in the Bible, Chapter 9) but nevertheless I think it was fitting that I walked through his home town with a donkey!

Paul's journey and letters make up a substantial part of the New Testament.

From Tarsus, it was only about twenty miles to Mersin.

I was nearly by the sea again, Hooray.

But when I approached Mersin the next day, I became disappointed.

It was an industrial town, so I just kept walking on and headed for a small town, called Silifke, which is sixty miles south west of Mersin.

The walk along the coast road to Silifke was pleasant and quite quaint in parts. It was wonderful to be next to the sea again and about fifty miles out into that sea was the island of Cyprus.

I had reached the Mediterranean coast ahead of time, and still had two weeks left on my Turkish visa. This somehow took the edge off my need to leave Turkey and go to Cyprus, but I still needed to organise the end of my walking trip with Sophie, so my plan was to find someone who showed a genuine look of concern for her and whoever that person turned out to be, I was going to give them Sophie as a free gift.

It was very common that the two of us got a lot of attention from people, but it was rare for someone to show real love or concern for Sophie. It wasn't a country where people did that sort of thing. Donkeys were a beast of burden, and that's as far as it usually went.

I reached the coastal town of Silifke and needed to buy some food from a small shop by the side of the road. A family from the shop and a few other people nearby started to gather around very quickly as usual.

The family that owned the shop were nice people and I noticed the young boy of the family was stroking Sophie and being nice to her, he must have been about nine years old.

He actually seemed fond of her.

I had found the new owner!

I indicated to the family, that I wanted to give Sophie to their son and I made it clear by hand signals that I didn't want any money.

They were amazed.

And the boy couldn't believe it. I started to unload the few personal belongings that I would need, but everything else like the saddle, basket, water containers, tent plastic, ropes and cooking stuff, I placed in a pile on the floor for the family to take as well.

Then the boy and I walked Sophie to a plot of grassland with some small trees. The family must have owned the land and it was to be where Sophie could, at last, stop her epic walk.

We had walked about nine hundred miles together. From the border of Greece (near Bulgaria), down to Istanbul, along the coast of the Black Sea and right down through the interior of Turkey, to the shore of the Mediterranean Sea. I had taken her from a tough gypsy camp existence and put her into the hands of someone who would love looking after her.

I hope she thought the walk was worth it!

She had done well and now deserved a long rest.

It was sad to say goodbye to her, but I didn't break down weeping, she was too busy enjoying the nice green grass to notice anyway!

Like most transitions in life, it wasn't long before I was navigating a new set of circumstances and the old circumstances were fading as quick as an early morning mist.

Within a few hours I was on a bus. My new form of transport was a lot quicker and didn't require as much from me, except of course the fare!

All of a sudden, I wasn't the strange traveller with a donkey. Now I was just a western-looking guy on a bus. Hardly worth a second look. Which was useful, but also humbling.

I was travelling west along the south coast of Turkey, in an area of Turkey where European travellers and even tourists could be spotted. Maybe it was going to be good to rub shoulders with some of them. I hadn't really had any conversations with people who spoke English since Semi, six weeks beforehand.

I reached Alanya and decided to hang out there for a couple of days. I even met a couple from England for a few hours and had some fun time together over a meal. We met up the next day also and they were intrigued about my walk across Turkey. Then they moved on and I was on my own again. It made me want more company and the next town I went to further along the coast I also stayed for a couple of days. There I met people from America and various European countries, people who spoke the English language.

But I was in the company of strangers and as time went on I started to feel alone even in the midst of fellow English speakers.

Maybe I had been on my own too long and socialising had become a bit of a lost art.

The solitude I had experienced 'on the road' had helped me get to know myself in a deeper way, but now among compatriots, I was struggling to know who I was.

I was feeling quite vulnerable, but had no one to confide in, no one who would understand my inner dilemma.

After about a week of this slow psychological downhill journey, I found myself in Fethiye, which was a beautiful remote coastal location with an inland lagoon.

It is now a very popular tourist location that is often shown on holiday brochures. But back then it was a bit of a secret.

Good-looking, hippy traveller-type people from around the world seemed to head there and hang out.

There was a friendly middle aged English guy running a cheap café joint near the beach. He was very gay and seemed to know the local scene inside-out. He was introducing myself and a guy from Germany called Matthew to the area, and as he led us along the sandy beach showing us good places to hang out, he said, 'Come and walk on the wild side.'

I could see it was a cool place to be, but I was struggling with the whole socialising scene.

No more Sophie to help me feel special.

I had planned on staying there for a few days, but it got to the point where I decided to leave Fethiye early the next morning without saying goodbye to the couple of people I had briefly got to know.

I was in quite a mess and feeling like I was on the edge. I had decided that the only way I was going to look after myself and my sanity was to not communicate with anyone at all. No interaction with any human being. Not even eye contact.

I was off, before sunrise.

I went into the main town, that was a mile or so inland and got on a bus going north to Izmir.

Izmir is a big seaport on the west coast and is the third biggest city in Turkey. It used to be named Smyrna and features in the book of Revelation at the end of the Bible.

A few days earlier I had bought a ticket for a ship journey from Izmir to Istanbul.

My plan was, to catch the magic bus from Istanbul to London.

I was due to arrive in Izmir, late in the afternoon, which would give me time to find a safe place to sleep.

About half way into the two-hundred-mile journey from Fethiye to Izmir the bus pulled into a busy bus station and everyone got off. I wasn't expecting this and guessed the bus had some sort of problem. The passengers were generally hanging around near the bus.

Because I was in such a state in my mind and emotions I walked over to a deserted bit of the bus park. I didn't want to interact with anyone while we waited for the bus to be fixed.

I occasionally glanced at the bus and the situation around it. I was holding myself together by being extremely self-contained. I was chained to my anchor of sanity by feeling confident that I was in control of the present situation going on around me.

But all of a sudden, that chain snapped, and my confidence was turned upside-down and thrown into a raging ocean of chaotic panic.

The bus had left.

My bag with all my belongings in, was still on board.

I was now forced to rush into the bus station building and try and engage with people behind the desk. An immediate crowd gathered round as I tried to communicate my situation, in a language no one understood.

It was the last thing I needed.

I was on the edge and now being chucked into a distressing situation. Even my jacket, traveller's cheques and passport were on that bus.

There were one or two people behind the desk that seemed to understand what I was trying to communicate.

Then someone arrived who spoke some English and I was told that they had phoned ahead to the Izmir bus station and they would send my stuff back on the first bus coming to the town where I was.

I would have to wait a few hours.

When a bus did eventually come back with my stuff, the sun had set and it had already started to get dark.

All my stuff was intact which was a huge relief, but I personally was far from being intact. This episode had shaken me to the core. What I mean by that is, I was no longer confident that I had control of situations around me. I was not anchored. I was adrift.

To make matters worse, I was getting on a late bus to a very big and unknown city.

When the bus pulled in at the Izmir bus station, I was feeling very vulnerable and self-conscious, and the area that I found myself in seemed to be in quite a dodgy neighbourhood.

As I walked around the back streets with my bag, looking for a suitable hotel, I felt like a little antelope surrounded by lions that were getting closer and closer, and they knew and I knew that there was no escape.

I was going to be taken out.

The hour was late but I managed to get myself a cheap hotel room for the night. It had just a single bed and a small wardrobe in it.

I shut the door to my room and breathed a little easier, but not much.

After a few minutes, I was in bed, but as I lay there I knew someone else was in the room with me, and it wasn't a good person.

There were only two places they could be: Under the bed... or in the wardrobe. I was scared.

I carefully looked under the bed and they weren't there. So, they had to be in the wardrobe.

I braced myself and tried to make myself feel strong, and quickly thrust open the wardrobe door.

But… there was no one there.

It was at that point I knew the devil was real and that he was in the room with me.

I was very frightened and I knew he knew. There was nothing I could do to hide. I was totally out of my depth.

I tried to go to sleep but I knew it was a farce pretending to him that I was tired. Somewhere inside me I was very tired, but that was relegated to the end of the queue now.

I felt like a pawn in a chess game.

I was caught between two powerful forces, much more powerful than me. I was neither on one side, or the other. And I had no peace whatsoever.

I lay there knowing there was a battle going on for my soul.

The next morning I went in search of another place to stay, hoping somehow to escape the evil presence I had been confronted with the night before.

I entered a few establishments and got some prices. As I entered one establishment, the man behind the desk put his hand over his heart as a gesture of kindness, but his price was higher than other places I had looked at, so I went with a cheaper one down the road, but of course, you get what you pay for!

The room I was taken to was right down in the basement. There were three other separate rooms down there, plus a shower/toilet room.

My room was extremely basic. It was the smallest bedroom I had ever been in. It was more like a doll's house. The room had one single bed, which 'just' fitted in. There was a foot gap along one side of the bed and that was the only bit of floor where you could stand. And I couldn't even stand up properly in the place, because I was too tall.

There was a tiny, little, one foot by one foot window, with no glass in it, which looked into the basement corridor. Privacy was provided, by a piece of old curtain, and the door was like a toy, so security was non-existent.

It was a joke situation.

But I was a million miles away from seeing it as a joke.

When I got in that small room, I just accepted it as my lot in life.

Life seemed to be getting worse by the hour and there was no way out of it. That was the only perspective I had.

I was so vulnerable from the night before that I couldn't even help myself get out of the situation.

I was paralysed with fear.

When I went to the toilet and looked in the shower room I had a premonition that I was going to end up dying in there, very soon, and that it was going to involve my Swiss army penknife in some way.

I had so much turmoil inside me, that even if I had been transported instantly to my family and best friends, they would not have been able to help me. I actually thought that very thought as the struggle continued.

Getting to England was not even worth contemplating. It would take nearly a week to get there even if I was 'all together'. I couldn't navigate it, mentally or emotionally.

The awareness of spiritual evil was beginning to consume me and I knew it was going to show up again more fully in the evening, like it had done the night before.

As I lay on that little bed around midday I was utterly convinced that things were going to turn out like I feared. I seemed to be hypersensitive to the evil that surrounded me.

I could hear a couple of men talking in Turkish in the small corridor in the basement. I knew that one of them was going to come to the little window in my wall and draw the cloth curtain to one side and look at me straight in the eyes. He was not going to be a good man and he was going to lock me into a stare. The mind-game-battle between him and I was going to be full on.

I needed to prepare myself because it was going to happen in only a few seconds time.

Sure enough, that man did come to my window as I lay on the bed quietly. He pulled the cloth curtain to one side and he looked right into my eyes and kept looking. And I just looked back at him.

He backed out after a few long seconds. I had only just held myself together.

That scary incident somehow slapped me around the face. It made me realise that I needed to get out of there and find another place to stay.

I remembered the man behind the desk at the small hotel up the street, who had made the kind gesture of putting his hand over his heart when I first met him.

I would go there.

I got my bag and jacket and made my way out of the basement. As I walked past the desk near the entrance, I saw the owner. I pointed downstairs and said in Turkish, 'Bad man.'

He was concerned… but I was gone.

I had paid for the night, but I didn't care about that. I needed to be safe.

I walked up the street to the other hotel. When I entered I saw the man I had negotiated with earlier in the morning and I put my hand over my heart.

He responded by doing the same.

He showed me the accommodation at the rear of the building, next to a little grassed garden courtyard. It was a simple but peaceful little room. I paid him for one night and he left me to make myself at home.

As I sat on the bed the sun broke through the clouds outside and shone on the side of my face.

I was in the right place.

Then all of a sudden, I knew what I had to do!

I had to get hold of a Bible.

It was early afternoon and my only mission in life was to get a Bible.

But where from? I was in a Muslim nation. Bibles were not what most Turkish people wanted in life.

I needed to find the British embassy.

As I walked along the streets I saw an expensive hotel that looked like it would cater for upmarket tourists. So, with that in mind I entered and found a lady at reception who could speak English.

I asked her where the British Embassy was and she informed me that there was only a British Consulate office in Izmir.

Well that will do I thought. They will have a Bible.

She showed me her map of the city and pointed out where the building was and she said, 'It's easy when you get near there because it's next to the church'.

Wow, there's a church.

Now I was on a new mission, to get to the church.

She explained roughly how I was to reach that area of the city, but as I went on my way, an urgency started riding up inside of me. I wasn't sure which way to go and on the few occasions I tried to ask people, they sent me in the wrong directions. It was like there was a spiritual war going on to prevent me getting to the church.

I was in a desperate state, so much so, that I could sense the devil telling me that I was not going to make it there and that I was going to lose my mind in the streets of this big city.

I really did feel again that I was a small antelope surrounded by lions.

It was like something out of 'The Exorcist' movie. Then as I got nearer to the area where the church was, the taunt changed to: 'Even if you get there, the door will be locked and you won't be able to get in.'

Then I saw the building in the distance. I quickened my pace and ran across a road, not even waiting for a break in the traffic.

There was a big metal gate separating the church path from the pavement and it was locked. I just climbed over it, in full view of the people nearby. I was beyond caring.

Then I ran to the big wooden church door. It was locked. I began to try and force it open, which alerted the attention of a Turkish man, who came round from the rear of a separate building next door.

He was concerned about what I was doing there and I indicated that I needed to get in the church. He could see that I was pretty desperate and seemed to be saying that I should follow him into his building, which was obviously nothing to do with the church.

So I followed him through a private yard and we entered the back door of the building.

He led me along a corridor to an office and behind the door of the office I could hear a man speaking to someone in English. As I listened again, I could hear that the man was British.

I think it dawned on me then that I was in the British Consulate building.

I could hear that he was on the phone but after about a minute I couldn't even wait for him to finish his phone call. I just opened the door and walked in and it turned out to be the exact instant he finished the call.

He was alarmed at my entrance, stood up, and said quite sternly, 'What are you doing in my office?'

'I need a Bible.'

'Who are you and where have you come from?'

I then took out my passport and all my travellers cheques (over £1000), put them on his desk and said, 'It's all yours, I need a Bible.'

I was definitely desperate!

He then said again in the same stern voice, 'I haven't got a Bible. Who are you?'

At that point I started to cry and break down.

His attitude suddenly changed and he said, 'It's OK, I have got a Bible.'

He turned around and got a large black Bible from the shelf behind him, and as he handed it to me he said, with a concerned tone, 'Do you want to be in a quiet room by yourself?'

I just nodded my head.

He then showed me to the room next to his office and assured me that I would be left alone.

I didn't really know what to do once I was in the room on my own.

I just sat on a chair and hugged the Bible to my chest.

Then a strange thing started to happen to my head and the ends of my arms and it took my attention. It was like a low charge of electricity. I was worried about it because it was like nothing I had ever felt before, and I couldn't stop it happening.

Then a thought process started up in my mind: 'I must be dying! My body, my mental state and my emotions are so totally spent, that my body is now on the edge of packing in. This must be what happens to people when they die, but we never hear about it because then they die and can't tell us what it feels like.'

But then another thought interrupted that original thought.

And this new thought was somehow dropped in my mind without me asking for it. It just popped into my awareness and said, 'Well when did the strange feeling start happening?'

And I realised that it had started happening when I put the Bible to my chest. I then looked at the Bible and thought to myself, 'Well this book has got something to do with good.'

I knew that from my childhood.

So... I decided to just let.

I know that is a strange sentence, but that is the only way I can explain perfectly what I did.

I just **let** it happen. I allowed it to happen. I in effect said yes to it.

And the moment that I made that decision, the experience started to travel down my arms, down from my head into my torso and then down through my legs to my feet.

And I was left sitting in that same chair with that same Bible, *but*, there was one thing that had changed.

I was now sitting there in... total peace.

I almost want to have a pause in the book at this point to allow respect for that moment. To just keep writing does not give that moment justice!

[   ]

I have just stopped writing... but you won't know that because I guess you're just reading on.

I understand that. You weren't in the room on that day. You are excused!

It was gigantically massive. It was actually a total miracle from heaven because it was so immediate and so thoroughly complete.

It was such a distinct crossover from one thing to another that I can only describe the immediacy of it in terms of a black piece of paper meeting a white piece of paper. There is a fine line of crossover from being in one section, to that of being in the next section. Being totally in one section and then finding myself totally in the other, was crazy.

I was in black… and then… I was in white.

All that had been going on inside of me when I entered that room had been totally flushed out of my body, mind, emotions and spirit.

And God's Spirit had come in. To take its place.

I just sat there in peaceful amazement.

I can't remember how long I sat there, but eventually I thought of opening the Bible and reading something.

I just opened it at random and the first thing I read was about a king called Nebuchadnezzar who had had dreams and his mind was so troubled that he couldn't sleep.

It just jumped out at me. I didn't even read anymore. It was God telling me that He knew what I had been going through.

In the office next door I could hear the British man on the phone to someone and the conversation was about me.

It transpired that he was phoning the chaplain of the Anglican church next door.

Within ten minutes the Chaplain, who was called Geoffrey, turned up at the office. I asked him if I could go into the church and was hoping that I would be left alone in there to continue my interaction with God, but both of the men stayed with me. I was still overwhelmed by everything that had happened to me. The difference it was going to make in my life from that day on would be profound.

I'm sure it was quite strange for those two men, having someone turn up the way I did: not a part of their everyday routine!

When it came for me to leave and say goodbye, I asked them if I could take the Bible with me. I knew I was very needful of it at that time. They understood and let me keep it, but I promised to mail it back to them one day (which later in the year I did).

I made my way back to the area of Izmir where I had come from and managed to locate the small street where I was staying. I again sat on the bed, this time knowing my life had totally changed, forever.

Quite instinctively I took my earring out of my ear lobe. It had a strange blue and white object I had bought in the Istanbul bazaar hanging from it. I chucked both things in the bin. Somehow, I didn't want or need an earring any more.

That night as I lay on my bed I knew I had to get out of Turkey the next day.

I had a ticket to go on a sea voyage round the west coast of Turkey and up through the Sea of Marmara to Istanbul, but that was never going to be used now. I needed to get back to England and find some Christians. Christians that would understand my story and not be phased when I talked about the devil and a battle for my soul.

That night I went to bed peacefully, with the Bible under my pillow.

The next morning, I left the place where I was staying and didn't book for the following night. I was on a mission to get an air ticket back to England.

And I had made a pledge to God: 'I was not going to eat anything until I was randomly offered it, by loving and understanding Christians, back in England.'

I walked around the city streets looking for travel agencies. By mid-afternoon I had found out that the only ticket available on the flight leaving that evening to London was an expensive business class ticket. The flight was to stop briefly in Munich.

Now buying an expensive ticket like that was not what I liked to do... but... I bit the bullet.

I handed over the money.

That in itself, was a miracle, let me tell you!

When I was on the plane and in the business class section I was offered all sorts of nice food and drinks. But I didn't take anything, my pledge still stood.

On the flight, God reminded me of my biker friend who had become a Christian, a year earlier.

Her name was Karen and she had gone off to a place called Lee Abbey to live. I presumed she must be a nun.

I had no idea where Lee Abbey was, but I felt God was prompting me to go and find it, because the people there would understand what I had been through.

The plane landed at Heathrow airport in the late evening. The terminal was quiet when I arrived. It was good to be back on English soil, but there was drama, even before I left the building.

The customs police officers pulled me over to one side and took me into a private room. There were three men and one woman. It was all very official and serious. I had come from Turkey and they were certain that I looked dodgy and was bringing drugs into the country.

It hadn't occurred to me at the time, but they may also have known I had been in business class.

Anyway, they were going through every little bit of my belongings. The woman was even reading through my diary journal! Then someone pulled a smallish paper sachet from one of the side pockets of the army bag I had. The sachet was in a poor state, had no writing on it and when they tore it open, it was full of a greenish coloured powder.

They asked, 'What is this then??'

I didn't recognise it at all and immediately thought, with absolute shock, 'Oh no they've planted drugs in my bag.'

I said, 'Why are you doing this? I don't believe it!'

Then they said again, 'Well, what is it?'

As I looked more closely at it I realised what it was.

I said, in an exultant tone, 'I know what it is! It's green dye, I bought it in Edirne to dye some shorts, but I forgot all about it. You can do all the tests you want on it: it's green dye.'

It had been a brief interlude in the proceedings.

They asked what I was doing in Turkey and why I was there. So, I started telling them I had bought a donkey and walked hundreds of miles through the country. They of course had many questions!

Then I was left alone with the main customs police officer.

He sat me down, looked intently at me and said in a very serious voice, 'I have been doing this job for many years and I know for certain you are bringing drugs in.'

I told him I wasn't, and that if he knew my story he would understand my appearance and why I was looking on edge.

I told him that it would take ages to tell him who I was and what I had been through in Turkey.

He said with the same sternness as before, 'I've got all night!'

So basically, I gave him a synopsis of my life before I had gone to Turkey and what had led me to want to go travelling on my own.

After about twenty minutes I reached the part when God made himself real to me for the first time, on the road in northern Turkey.

As I was pouring my heart out to him I started to relax and sense that I was portraying well who I was, and what had been happening in my life. I started to feel safe in that interrogation room. Now, because I was more relaxed, I felt it was OK to release some built-up wind in my stomach. Silently out... and into the universe!

A few seconds later, with me at a truly deep part of the story and him intently listening, the atmosphere in the room was abruptly interrupted with the words, 'Have you just farted?'

I couldn't believe it. I was telling him my innermost secrets and he was put off by a smell.

I said, 'Yeah...so what?!'

'There's only one reason you have released wind and that's because you have a container of drugs in your stomach.'

I then said with indignation, 'Well you're wrong!'

He then left the room.

I waited for maybe ten minutes, then another guy came in and said, 'You can go now.' I was surprised and very relieved.

I packed all my stuff up, but I didn't want to leave. I wanted to see the man that had been listening to my story. I needed to ask him something before I could leave the airport in peace.

I waited near the room for about a minute or two and then I heard a door open further along the corridor. It was him and he was putting on his coat, ready to leave the building. I waited for him to reach where I was waiting and I said timidly, 'Did what I was saying to you in there make sense?'

And he gently replied, 'Yeah, it did.'

I looked at him, 'Thank you.'

And then we went our separate ways. I now had strength. I had been heard and most importantly, had been understood.

I could now venture out into the next chapter, to get a train to Torquay.

It was strange to be back in England, after months away. I had been on a very secret, life-changing adventure and England was now new to me, in so many ways.

I navigated the next part pretty smoothly, apart from a comical incident with a London taxi cab driver outside Victoria train station.

A railway worker at Victoria railway station had informed me that Paddington railway station was the one I needed in order to get a train to Torquay, and that the last one that night would leave in about fifteen minutes.

So I ran out of Victoria station and hailed a London taxi cab. Through the front passenger door window I asked the driver if he could get me to Paddington train station in ten minutes. He was a real cockney geezer. He said he could and told me to jump in.

So, I opened the front passenger door, chucked my bag on the floor and got in.

In those black taxicabs the driver is separated from the passenger area by a piece of glass.

Now, I went to sit down next to him but there was no seat!

Because I was in a world of my own and was intent on reaching Paddington in time, I just thought it a bit strange, but knelt down on the floor anyway. I held the dashboard with both hands, looked forward and said, 'OK, let's go!'

After a couple of seconds, I was aware that he wasn't pulling away. I then heard the words, 'We're going nowhere with you knelt there.'

'What do you mean?'

'You're in the luggage compartment, until you go and sit in the seats behind, we're going nowhere.'

I quickly opened the door, got out and entered the cab through the door behind. Then I was in the land of seats!

I apologised and explained that I had been abroad and wasn't really acquainted with London cabs because I had lived in Devon for years! He informed me that the sealed off compartment was for suitcases and large luggage. Then I saw the funny side of it (as I still do now!) He loosened up after a few minutes into the trip and got me to Paddington in time to catch the train to Torquay.

I arrived at the main Torquay station about the time the dawn chorus was setting up. Birds waking and singing in the new day, as the light started to overtake the darkness. Nice time to arrive.

It was too early to go to my parent's house, which was a five-minute walk from the station. The sea is just across the road from Torquay train station and it was the obvious place to go and contemplate my return to recognised normality.

I walked to the nearby Corbyn head viewpoint that looks out over the bay.

I was back in my safe and known, home territory. As I stood there, at the break of day, I realised that I was at a very important juncture in my life.

I had a choice to make:

Choice 1:

I could step back into my old way of existence and melt back into the same social circuit I had been in before I left England. If I did that, I could be an ego party-wizard, charged up by all the adventures I had had while I was away and it would be fun for a while; but alongside that choice was the realisation that I would have to mute my excitement about how God had made Himself so real to me and given me a whole new perspective on life.

That type of talking would not be tolerated for too long alongside the type of living that I would slip back into with my old friends.

Yes, I would have to keep quiet about God, let that experience fade away in the past and ultimately leave it where I found it.

Or

Choice 2:
Keep walking forward in this new adventure; keep hanging onto my faith in God; find out where Lee Abbey was; go there and hopefully meet other Christians who would have empathy with my experience; learn more about the Christian faith and probably join a church.

It was the junction where I could take the blue pill or the red pill. There was no middle ground.

It was all or nothing. Deny it ever happened or proclaim it and live fully.

It didn't take too long to decide. Less than thirty seconds.

I couldn't deny to myself what had happened out in Turkey. God had truly saved me. I needed saving. I had been in a mess, if I was honest, for most of my life.

I had left England looking for answers; looking for real Life.

If I denied what I'd found, where else was there to go?!

God had revealed what life was all about. The searching had ended.

It was futile to go any other way than forward. My decision was made.

Marriage... was the only way forward.

Marriage to... GOD!

The sun had risen and I started walking to my parent's house. What would they think of me suddenly turning up out of nowhere?

I had been gone for nearly five months. When I left, it was an open-ended ticket into the future, with no real plan of returning.

My Mum's last words to me as I walked away from their house in Goshen Road were, 'I hope you find what you're looking for Mark.' There was concern in her eyes when she said it.

I had sent a postcard after I had bought Sophie, so they had known I was in Turkey, but that was the last contact I had made with them.

As I walked to their house I still had the big black Bible tucked inside my jacket. I had been holding it close to me all the way from Izmir. It was a lifeline and I was hanging on tight.

I walked up the small rear garden path to the house and finding the door was still locked, I sat on the doorstep and just quietly waited.

The house was an old terraced house, with a basement kitchen. The kitchen door opened onto the small rear garden.

I was quite nervous as I sat on the rear doorstep. How on earth was this going to unfold?

After about ten minutes, I could hear my dad walking down the interior staircase to the basement kitchen. Then I heard him unlocking the rear door to come out and smell the fresh air.

And there was I!

'Hi Dad.'

'Hello Mark, you're back!'

Dad could see something was heavily on my mind.

We went inside and I sat on a chair next to the kitchen table. Dad put the kettle on to make a pot of tea. He looked at me and probably wondered why I was not saying anything.

Thing was, I was preparing myself to say something.

I got the black Bible out from inside my jacket, put it on the table and said, 'Dad... this is what it's all about'

Then there was an uncomfortable silence.

After a few seconds, the reply came back, 'It's a good book, yes.'

Then more uncomfortable silence, that lasted longer than the first uncomfortable silence.

Dad had now sat down on the bottom step of the stairs leading up into the house.

It was quite a few moments before anyone next spoke.

We were both now sat down.

He slowly said, 'Mark, I just don't think as deep as you.'

I turned my head round to him, he looked up at me and I said, 'Dad, that's no excuse.'

And with that, his head dropped.

Nothing more was said.

After a few minutes, I asked where Mum was. Dad said she was just getting up. I walked up the two flights of stairs to their bedroom and knocked on the bedroom door.

'Mum, it's me, Mark.'

Mum was dressed and opened the door. She immediately could see that I was concerned about something. I went in and sat on the bed. She sat down next to me.

'How are you?' she said, sounding quite concerned.

I just sat there, quietly, looking at the ground.

Then I pulled the Bible out from inside my jacket again and said, 'Mum, this is what it's all about.'

The reply came… 'I knew you'd find it in the end.'

Then I cried and Mum put her arm around me.

I had no idea that Mum was going to say that, but it was a deep tonic to my soul.

I had come home – in more ways than one!

Over twenty years after this event, I was lying in bed one morning and I remembered the little song that I used to sing, while walking on my own in Turkey – 'What's it all about – I really wanna know?'

And then I remembered the words that I had spoken to my parents when I first got back to England and put the Bible in front of them – 'This is what it's all about.'

I never knew God even existed when I was singing that song. I was just singing it around the void of my head, as I walked along.

But twenty years later God showed me that I had answered that song from Turkey with the statement to my parents.

My next mission was to find out where Lee Abbey was.

I looked in the telephone directory for the first Christian organisation I could see and phoned them. I wanted to find out where Lee Abbey was! The person who answered the phone had heard of Lee Abbey and told me that it was on the North Devon coast, near Lynton.

I was surprised that it was in the same county as me – Devon. That would make things easier!

I was still not eating anything, my pledge to God back in Izmir was not taken lightly; I was not going to eat anything until I was randomly offered it, by loving and understanding Christians, back in England.

It was pretty full-on as I look back on it, but it was something I needed to do at the time. I still felt I was in a battle. I had reached the other side so to speak, but I needed to stay on the other side!

(Mum's faith had taken a back seat in a lot of ways since leaving Surrey in the early '70s. The more hectic lifestyle of running the hotel and restaurant in Chudleigh had occupied a lot of her time, although she and dad did take us to church periodically, usually against our wills! Since moving to Torquay they never really bothered, they pretty much kept themselves to themselves.)

Mum was concerned that I wasn't eating and her nursing background kicked in. She wanted our local doctor to come and see me before I went off in search of this 'Lee Abbey.'

I said I didn't need a doctor, but to keep the peace I agreed to her phoning him.

What I didn't know at the time, but found out later, was that the Consulate in Izmir had got my parents phone number from the back of my passport and phoned them after I had left the Consulate.

The chaplain and the official there, had said they were concerned about my health. Probably my mental health!

So, the doctor arrived at the house, sat down in the sitting room and faced his patient – me!

He asked me general questions about my travels and then moved on to the spiritual side of things.

He wasn't too keen on my belief that the devil really existed, and not so excited about the existence of God either. So, we sat on different sides of the fence there.

Then he checked my blood pressure and a few other things.

At the end of all the proceedings, he didn't hospitalise me, so I lived to fight another day!

In the evening I phoned directory enquiries and got the Lee Abbey phone number; then I phoned Lee Abbey and spoke to a guy about my age called Chris. I told him that I had been walking through Turkey with a donkey and found God!

I discussed the need for me to visit Lee Abbey and he was very encouraging and told me to just come.

The next morning, I got myself together for the new unknown adventure ahead.

As I was leaving the house my mum, still very concerned about my wellbeing, tried to persuade me to have at least a drink of orange juice, but I reminded her that I needed to do what I needed to do.

She reluctantly let me go, again, hoping I would find what I was looking for.

I had looked on a map and Lynton was on the edge of Exmoor about twenty miles from Barnstaple, so I boarded a train from Torquay to Exeter and from there I would make my way to Barnstaple.

I had taken some spare clothes in a bag with me, because I was hoping that the people at Lee Abbey would let me stay for a while. I was prepared to just sleep in a field, as long as I was around Christians.

Karen, my old biker friend, would be there and also Chris who I had spoken to on the phone. Presumably, they would both be wearing religious order clothing – some kind of plain coloured habit.

I was going to be entering a whole new world!

Maybe I would become a monk…

I didn't mind what job I did in the future, even the most mundane job would be fine, now I knew God.

I had forgotten to mention to Chris that I knew Karen, so she was going to have a big surprise, with me turning up at Lee Abbey!

At Exeter I waited a while and eventually got on a train to Barnstaple. I was getting more nervous as I got nearer to North Devon.

What if Lee Abbey didn't have time for me? Maybe they would reject me and send me on my way!

I didn't have any plan B.

Plan A was all I had and if it failed, I was on my own. I didn't want to be on my own, I needed to be understood and loved.

It was all very desperate really!

I still remember the anxiety I had, even now as I write.

Barnstaple was the end of the line concerning my train journey.

It was now the turn of buses to transport me.

I walked across the medieval long bridge over the River Taw and found the bus station on the other side.

There was a bus going to Lynton in less than an hour. As I waited at the bus station I saw that the number of the bus going to Lynton was 666.

I sort of took it in my stride, because that was the spiritual stride I was in, but it still rattled me. Where was I going?!

Bus number 666 arrived, I got on and soon I was on my way to Lynton.

The bus trundled through the autumn countryside. It was late September and the multicoloured beauty of my home country stood in sharp contrast to the drier landscapes I had been recently wandering about in.

When the bus reached Lynton, I was sort of in another country, within my own country.

North Devon had a different feel about it.

Lynton is on the cliff shoreline of the Bristol channel and looks across to Swansea and the Brecon Beacons in South Wales.

Lee Abbey was only a mile or so along the coast from Lynton. I had to walk the last part of the journey.

The route took me through 'The Valley of the Rocks'. It is quite obvious when you are there why it is so named. It was a dramatic setting for my exit from one world, into another.

As I walked along through the valley, my mind wrestled with the possible scenarios I would be confronted with when I crossed over into the Lee Abbey estate at the other end.

As the Valley of the Rocks came to its end, I passed a sign by the road that informed me that the large rock looming over me to the left was called the 'devil's knife'.

Even at that late point there was still the rattling of the sabre, as it were, to try and unnerve me about leaving the world that I had always known and entering fully into this new life that was now inside me. But I kept focusing forward, with literally the gateway in front of me.

This 'new world' that I was about to enter was where I wanted to belong. Whether it came up to the mark or not, I was very soon to find out.

Little did I know – some unexpected shocks were just around the corner…

To be continued…

final word (for now)

The events that have followed that period of my life back in 1985 have continued to be an adventure, but of a different kind. For the last 33 years my adventures have not been experienced on my own. They have been led by and lived with my God, who has been my best friend and my Rock.

The bible verses that best explain my God experience out in Turkey are from Psalm 18 verses 1 – 6 and 16 – 19:

I love you, Lord, my strength.
The Lord is my rock, my fortress and my deliverer;
my God is my rock, in whom I take refuge,
my shield and the strength of my salvation, my stronghold.
I called to the Lord, who is worthy of praise,
and I have been saved from my enemies.
The cords of death entangled me;
the torrents of destruction overwhelmed me.
The cords of the grave coiled around me;
the snares of death confronted me.
In my distress I called to the Lord;
I cried to my God for help.
From his temple he heard my voice;
my cry came before him, into his ears.

He reached down from on high and took hold of me;
he drew me out of deep waters.
He rescued me from my powerful enemy,
from my foes, who were too strong for me.
They confronted me in the day of my disaster,
but the Lord was my support.
He brought me out into a spacious place;
he rescued me because he delighted in me.
(NIV version)

The title of this book is a bit of a deliberate play on words because although I did travel from Torquay to faraway places on the other side of the world like Australia, Japan and Alaska, it wasn't to the end of the world. Because the earth is round and you can't reach the end of the world as such. 😊

But I did, in another way, come to the end of the world!

Let me explain; in 1 John 2 verses 15 – 17 it reads:

Stop loving this evil world and all that it offers you, for when you love the world, you show that you do not have the love of the Father in you. For the world offers only the lust for physical pleasure, the lust for everything we see, and pride in our possessions. These are not from the Father. They are from this evil world. And this world is fading away, along with everything it craves. But if you do the will of God, you will live forever.
(NLT version)

And in John 15 verse 19 Jesus says:

'The world would love you as one of its own if you belonged to it, but you are no longer part of the world. I chose you to come out of the world...'
(NLT version)

But of course I still live in the world (on planet Earth), but I have come out of the ways of the world and its mentality. I came to the end of living in those ways.

After a few days at Lee Abbey I was led back to Torquay. But things would be very different. I was to live a whole new life. I suppose a bit like when a caterpillar dies, it comes out of the chrysalis as a whole new thing, and it begins to fly!

It is born again into a whole new way of living.

This is what Jesus speaks of in John 3 verse 3:

'I tell you the truth, no-one can see the kingdom of God unless he is born again.'
(NIV version)

So hopefully you get the idea of what I am trying to portray here.

If you are interested in reading about *how deep the rabbit hole went after I got out of the matrix*, see over the next page.

Also if you want to contact me anytime:

markalex.wadie@gmail.com

Thanks for reading this one. I feel as if you know me now!

I also want to thank Julia, Charles and... Alex (my wife; you will find out about her in the next instalment) for reading through this and making alterations and suggestions.

Also thanks to Charles & Jana for lending me their house in the Isle of Man last year to write this in solitude.

And to the Living Hope church in Port St Mary (Isle of Man) for being hospitable to me when I walked down to their office some days.

Also thanks to Dave Hopwood who has helped me to get this self-published. I first met Dave on that day I walked into Lee Abbey back in September 1985. We have stayed in contact since the Eighties.

Here is a promise for any of you out there who are searching for the meaning of life:

Jesus says this to you in Matthew 7 verses 7 – 8:

'Ask and it will be given to you; seek and you will find; knock and the door will be opened to you. For everyone who asks receives; the one who seeks finds; and to the one who knocks, the door will be opened.'
(NIV version)

So for now, goodbye, and lots of love.

Mark

'May the Lord bless you and protect you.
 May the Lord smile on you and be gracious to you.
 May the Lord show you his favour and give you peace.'

Numbers 6 verses 24 – 26
(NIV version)

See over the page for the next part of Mark's story...

Published in July 2019, the sequel is now available –

Torquay ... After the End of the World:

A godless world is always demanding attention.

At first it seems to be the way but then it spends you out. No loose change is left. The pocket of the soul is emptied, leaving a dry and barren place.

World, world, world where is your refreshment? Where is the satisfaction you promise? I'm still dry, dry. Where is your water? Your streams don't reach me, even when I drink. I swallow but it seeps away.

You don't keep your word. You tempt me with your smile; you caress me with your body; you move me with your beat; and you say, "Don't miss out. I'm here for you right now."

But on a clear day, world, I can see right through you. I can see behind your back and you're a liar, world – it's just a clever act.

Behind your back there's death.

This book is the sequel to :
'Torquay ... to the End of the World'

Torquay ... After the End of the World

Mark Wadie

Torquay ... After the
End of the World

Mark
Wadie

Printed in Great Britain
by Amazon

86378469R00149

Disciples of Ishq

AN INSIGHT ON TRUE LOVE'S FORGOTTEN CREED

Syed Arslan Ali Zaidi

ISBN-10: 1976080037
ISBN-13: 978-1976080036

DEDICATION

All praise is due to Allah ﷻ, the Lord of the Worlds. The Beneficent, the Merciful. Master of the Day of Judgement. Allah ﷻ's Peace and Blessings be upon His Final Messenger ﷺ, his pure family, his noble Companions, and all those who follow them with righteousness until the day of Judgement.

This book is dedicated to the thousands of avid readers on Instagram that enjoyed reading my thoughts, and through their love and encouragement have made me believe in myself. Moreover, I would like to take the opportunity to thank Nazaneen Kaliwal and Sadaf Gani for their hard work in editing this book. If it hadn't been for you all, this book would not have been a possibility.

They asked me who I loved.
I gave them a hundred names.
Ninety-nine of whom I prayed to,
and of the only one I prayed for.

Arslan Zaidi
09-30-15

CONTENTS

Acknowledgements

ACKNOWLEDGMENTS

I owe an enormous debt of gratitude to my best friends Nazaneen Kaliwal and Laraib Yasin Chaudhry. Through the struggles and trials of becoming the writer and the person that I have inevitably evolved into, both have been a constant source of inspiration and motivation. Thank you. Furthermore, I would like to thank all of the friends that have encouraged me to reach my potential in one way or another. From Stephen Leacock C.I.: Bushra Wali, Sajjad Jaffer, Hamza Asghar, Imran Kabir, Youlanne Barrette, Mansi Lakhani, Nishita Nayyar, Raza Naqvi, Sahl Syed, Arslan Khan, Ramani Jeya, Sohail Ahmed, Ayah Abdullah, Ateet Kapadia, Ebrahim Goralwala. From my years at York University: Bilal Anjum, Saad Suleman, Usman Baig, Raza Rahman, Nabeela Ahmed, Kamra Khalid, Shilpika Nathaniel, Zain Rizvi, Aliza Rizvi, Hayla Amini, and the incredible Teaching Assistant, Vanessa Rosa for her help with my Law School application. I would especially like to thank Saad Suleman and his blessed family for being an extended family of my own when I needed one. Thank you Suleman Uncle, Sabeen Aunty, Fahad and Maham for accepting me into your home. From City University of London: Bilawal Khan and Mustafa Khan. Moreover, a thank you to the remainder of my friends who have been like a family to me, Najeeb Abro, Bilal Khan, Rohan Saeed, Ahsan Ashraf, Anila Malik, Amalka Zainab, Ammar Rizvi, Kainat Ahmad, Sophia Javed, Kiran Khan, Tanveer Ahmed Khan, Omar Wynne, Romana Ephraim, Asma Waheed, Areeba Waheed, Waqas Rafiq. Furthermore, special thanks to the writers, friends, and family of Instagram for their precious feedback and encouragement: My sister Carla Choufany, Kainat Ali Khan, Muzna Shabbir, Arooba Malik, Sadaf Gani, Marghalara Khan, Azeema Ilyas, Hira Nazir, Shab Ujala, Mahwish Azhar, Mahnoor Bajwa, Bina Awan, Filza Ahmed, Sitara Jat, Ibrahim Abdul, Talha Shaikh, Zahira Javaid, Suvaiba Ahmed, Shamaz Khan, U.F. Shah, Faisal Nazir, Faisa Mahmud, Zaibun-Nissa Butt, KalelWrites (Mohammad), Saira Mahmood, Filza Ahmed, Muhammad Yahya, Maliha, Afifa Umair, Asiya Sakhalkar, Alisha Ali, Bilal and Zainab, along with the thousands of followers that constitute Team Arslan. Lastly, I would like to thank my family for their support that has never allowed me to give up. Thank you Mamma, Baba, Rukhsar, Tariq, Haiya, Raza and the little ones; Anaya, Azaan and Kainat. I love you guys. Lastly, a big thanks to Iqra Chisti for inspiring the front cover design.